To Bruce Thompson —

May all your bulls come big and EASY! :)

Jim Bunch
1/10/99

How to Get an
EASY ELK

By
JIM ZUMBO

With a Foreword by
Patrick F. McManus

All photos by the author unless otherwise noted.

Jacket and book design by Nancy L. Doerrfeld-Smith

Cover painting by famed cowboy humor artist, **Boots R. Reynolds**. Boots' artwork has appeared in many magazines such as Western Horseman, Horse and Horseman, and Horse and Rider. His originals and prints are displayed in many western galleries and carried by the SageBrushes Company, Sandpoint, Idaho. Boots resides with his wife, Becky in their mountain home near Hope, Idaho.

Copyright © 1998 by Jim Zumbo

All rights reserved, including the right to reproduce this book or any part thereof, in any form or media, except for inclusion of brief quotations in a review.

ISBN: 0-9624025-6-7

Published by:
Jim Zumbo
Wapiti Valley Publishing Company
P.O. Box 2390
Cody, Wyoming 82414
(307) 587-5486, 1-800-673-4868
http://www.jimzumbo.com

Dedication

*For my wife, Madonna,
who makes it all happen.*

Contents

Introduction

Chapter		Page
1	Why Elk Hunting Isn't Easy	1
2	You Can Buy an Easy Elk	7
3	You Can Win an Easy Elk	21
4	Luck May Get You an Easy Elk	27
5	How Not to Get an Easy Elk	33
6	Make Your Elk Hunt Easier	37
7	What Makes an Elk Tick	45
8	Elk Country Isn't User Friendly	53
9	The Easiest Elk of All	59
10	The Easiest Bull of All	65
11	Everything You Wanted to Know About Outfitters	71
12	You Can Hunt Elk for $500	85
13	The Do-It-Yourself Hunt	91
14	The Truth About Ranch Hunting	101
15	The Basics of Calling	105
16	In the Trenches for Elk	115
17	Go Late for an Easy Elk	125
18	Hunting Strategies That Work	133
19	Get It Out of the Woods	145
20	The Good Old Days Are Right Now	159
21	The Future of Hunting	167
	Appendix: Where to Find Your Easy Elk	173

Foreword

Jim Zumbo thinks like an elk. Although that may be something of a handicap when working long division, it comes in mighty handy when hunting elk — and when writing a book on hunting elk.

Experienced elk hunters may find the title a bit suspect. Easy elk? Do they really exist? Is Zumbo pulling our leg? As he indicates in his introduction, even Jim is a little suspicious of the title. But, as he explains, there really are easy elk, at least if you accept his definition: An easy elk is one that is dead and tagged. Up to that point, of course, it could be the orneriest, cunningest, most miserable beast ever to set hoove on a mountain.

Oh sure, there actually are a few easy elk out there, if you happen to be extremely lucky. In one instance, a hunter who did absolutely everything wrong that a hunter could possible do wakes up from a nap to see his elk ambling toward him. He shoots it next to the road and hauls it back to camp, to the amazement and dismay of his hard-hunting but elkless buddies.

This book covers just about all the bases as far as elk hunting is concerned. There is even a chapter for the obese, handicapped and out-of-shape hunter. Why Zumbo would devote an entire chapter to me I have no idea. Still, I found it useful, and I appreciate it. One of the tips for elk hunters such as I is to get yourself driven to the top of a mountain and hunt down. Then your partner picks you up that evening on the road below. Or he forgets to pick you up and goes home, something Zumbo forgot to mention. Still, this is a very practical way to hunt, particularly if you are after an easy elk and in no hurry for supper.

What's the hardest elk? Zumbo says those residing in the rain forests of the Pacific Northwest. There the hunter can expect to spend a good part of the day fighting his way through thickets of devils clubs, crawling about on hands and knees to get past fallen trees, and peering through shade as dark as night. He says the underbrush is so dense it could repel a snake. "Add to all this a lot

of water, and I mean a lot of water, in the form of rain, fog, and drizzle, and you have one of the toughest chunks of elk country on the planet."

Easy Elk also goes into considerable detail on how not to get an elk, even an easy one. I have personally tested each of the techniques mentioned and can assure you that they all work for not getting an elk.

Zumbo has hunted elk so much he bugles in his sleep. It is probable he has personally experienced every conceivable situation an elk hunter might find himself in — while hunting elk, that is. It is this personal experience in so many different situations that makes Jim's instruction on elk hunting so valuable, both to the beginner and the old hand. The tips are illustrated with dozens of anecdotes from Zumbo's own hunts. The entertainment value alone is well worth the cost of the book, and also one of the reasons Jim is the most-read hunting writer in the country. Reading Zumbo is the next best thing to hunting with him, and a good deal less tiring. Get the book. That's the first step in finding your easy elk.

Patrick F. McManus

Introduction

Is there really such a thing as an easy elk, or am I purposely fibbing just to sell a bunch of books? The truth is, an easy elk truly exists, but is by far the exception rather than the rule. Perhaps the name of this book should really be, how to get an "easier" elk, all things being relative. Certainly the hunt itself as well as the obvious task of getting the large carcass out of the hills lends itself to plenty of work. A successful elk hunt is more often a physical ordeal than one that ends up with an unfilled tag. The old saying, "the fun of the hunt is over when you squeeze the trigger," is never truer than in elk country.

Another possible book title could be "How to Be a Successful Elk Hunter", incorporating all the aspects of elk hunting. This book, by necessity, will indeed address all the tenets of the hunt as well as the idiosyncrasies of the animal. There is no substitute for knowledge.

As you read on, you'll begin to understand that an easy elk is not necessarily one that requires no physical outlay (though I'll certainly explore that possibility in depth), but one that involves the mere triumph of finally adding your name to the roster of successful elk hunters. If you've hunted elk for five years and have yet to score, for example, and your first elk was taken by a new set of strategies you adopted, you might agree the challenge was "easy", but still be faced with transporting the critter two miles to a road. So it is that this book will detail every tiny aspect of elk hunting that will afford you success, even though every phase may not be technically easy. It will also describe how to make that two-mile journey to the road with your elk a bearable task, and not one that may induce a hernia, severe back pain, or worse, heart failure.

To many, an easy elk means a tagged, deceased elk, and nothing more. If you'll abide by that definition, this book will tell you where and how to increase your odds of finding your elk. It will also tell you where and how to locate a quality bull, keeping in mind the painful fact that many prime elk areas *have no* quality bulls.

On the other hand, if your definition of an easy elk is simply pulling the trigger without expending much physical effort, and having someone else dress and deliver your elk from the woods to a processing plant, then it's all here in this book as well. In that regard, I'll identify the pitfalls to such an endeavor, since many of those no-brainer, no-work hunts end up as being expensive nightmares.

I've spent most of a lifetime admiring, photographing, observing, and hunting elk. Few major mountain ranges in the west have not seen the bottom of my boots, and my mountain home in northwest Wyoming just outside Yellowstone Park allows me the opportunity to watch elk year round. Despite that time spent in the elk woods, I still learn something new every time I shoulder my rifle and head for the hills. The big animals are unpredictable, and are always teaching me new tricks, all of which are incorporated in this book.

I'm always looking for an easy elk, and every now and then I get one, however you define it. I hope you do, too. If so, then this book has been a success.

Elk live in a wide variety of habitats. One of the extremes is above timberline, where the air is thin and the slopes are steep.

Chapter 1

Why Elk Hunting isn't Easy

Picture this scene. You're hunting in a remote wilderness, the elk rut is at its peak, and you've never been more exhilarated on a hunt. Everything is absolutely perfect, and you just know you're going to get the Bull of the Woods. It's the first morning of the hunt, and you plan on taking your time. No sense rushing it, since you've got seven days to hunt.

Now it's the evening of the seventh day. You sit on your cot, staring at the tent wall. You pull your unpunched elk license out of your pocket and look at it. Maybe you should have it framed because it's the only thing going up on your wall. The hunt is over, and you have nothing to show for it but pictures and memories. Somehow the "perfect" hunt you envisioned never materialized. You try to rationalize and tell yourself that hunting doesn't necessarily mean you have to shoot something, but the disappointment lingers on, like a pesky sore throat.

The easy hunt you anticipated turned into a nightmare. The elk and weather didn't cooperate, and you feel like you've aged 10 years. The steep terrain was unforgiving, and the thick blowdowns practically defied travel. But at least you gave it everything you had, and you were pleased when the guides offered you a toast at dinner, welcoming you into the fraternity of elk hunters. You're blooded, even though you're going home empty, and now you know why elk hunting is called the mother of all tough hunts on the continent.

2 How to Get an Easy Elk

Veteran elk hunters chuckle when they hear me talking about getting an easy elk. "There are no easy elk," many of them say. As you'll see as you read this book, there truly are easy elk, but let's address the popular perception that elk hunting isn't easy.

An elk is a big critter. The routine chore of field-dressing and skinning the carcass can be a major task.

The most obvious problem in elk hunting is moving the carcass. This can be either a minor task or a Herculean effort that could cause serious injury. Just because you can drive to a downed elk, which is a rare event in steep, timbered. elk country, doesn't mean you can load it easily.

I recall a solo hunt I made a few years ago. I had a cow tag, and came upon a bunch of cows just crossing a road in front of me. I slipped out of the truck, walked to a handy log, used it for a rest, and downed the cow. She fell in a place where I was able to drive to her. Easy, right? What more could a guy ask for?

But then reality set in. This was a big cow, probably weighing 450 pounds. There was no way I could get the dressed carcass in the truck myself. I ended up cutting her in half, and still had a devil of a time lifting each half in. I messed up my back, which is easy to do, but nonetheless I was home by midmorning. It wasn't a tough hunt, but the loading process added the difficult part.

Why Elk Hunting Isn't Easy 3

The day before that hunt, I drew a bead on a big cow, but common sense luckily prevailed and I didn't squeeze the trigger. I'd hiked three miles from a trailhead, and if I shot the elk it would have taken me a day and a half, and a whole lot of physical effort, to get it out.

So it becomes readily apparent that transporting an elk can be a monumental job, even if it falls close to a road.

Other than the need to transport the carcass in some fashion, the big-time reason why elk hunting isn't easy is due to the nature of elk country itself. There's a chapter in this book describing elk country; suffice to say it is quite commonly the nastiest terrain in the west, especially in coastal forests where Roosevelt elk live. In most elk country, wherever you are in the west, you're dealing with timber and steep slopes. Those are the two important obstacles.

This is just an average bull, and the hunter was lucky enough to get it to camp in one piece. Imagine the job at hand if the bull fell in the bottom of Forgotten Canyon!

Here's yet another reason why elk hunting isn't easy. The animals are timber-oriented and are masters at hiding. Can you see this bull?

Add the scenario of few roads and trails to the steep, heavily timbered country, and you have a serious challenge not to be taken lightly. Rockslides, deep gorges, cliffs, rushing streams, roaring rivers, and heavy blowdowns are common in elk country, providing even more obstacles.

The difficulty of negotiating the landscape is bad enough, but when you consider that many *miles* of that country must often be traveled to find elk, then you're in for serious strain on your body.

Weather may also contribute negatively, fouling up your hunt in a big way. In elk country, you can expect the extremes — from heat waves to sub-zero temperatures. Roads may be temporarily closed because of deep snow and drifts, or hot weather can be so oppressive to elk that animals "jungle up" in dense thickets and blowdowns, coming out only at night to feed, if they come out at all.

If you're hunting in high elevations, which is common in the central Rockies such as Colorado, Utah, Wyoming, New Mexico, and parts of Montana and Idaho, you'll be breathing thin air, which can be unpleasant if you live near sea level. Altitude sickness is no fun, and may be one of the many reasons why elk will remain elusive.

The nature of elk doesn't help matters much, either. Foraging at night, they easily escape detection. They may do some feeding at first light and show up again just before dark, but not so if there are hunters around. You can bet elk will remain nocturnal.

And when they *are* in places that offer some visibility, their camouflaged pelts often conceal them if there are some shadows and brush around.

If you're hunting during the rut and assume that elk are pushovers for calls, then you're in for another surprise. Some animals do indeed respond very well, but many don't, preferring instead to remain silent or run off in the opposite direction.

So there, folks, are a bunch of reasons why elk aren't easy customers come fall. Each of these factors will be closely analyzed elsewhere in this book.

6 How to Get an Easy Elk

Jim Zumbo with the only bull he ever took on an Indian reservation. You can buy one of these hunts at a cost of $10,000 and up.

Chapter 2

You Can Buy an Easy Elk

It's no secret that money can buy most anything, including an elk. There are a number of possibilities here, if you have a generous bank account, and I'll detail each of them.

BUY IT FROM A GAME FARM

Scattered across the country are a fair number of game farms containing elk. These farms are also known as preserves or elk ranches. Whatever you call them, they have one thing in common: captive elk contained by a tall fence, usually eight feet high. Some of these farms are fairly extensive, encompassing several thousand acres, and some are much smaller.

If you must own an elk and have no interest in all the associated aspects of the wild hunt, you can buy an animal and shoot it in an enclosure. Note I said *shoot* and not *hunt* it. There is a world of difference. Comparatively speaking, this is the easiest elk you can get. You can fly into town, be whisked to the game farm, enter the enclosure and handily shoot your elk, write a check to the game farm operator, give him the details on how you want your elk mounted by a taxidermist, and be back on an afternoon plane without getting your shoes dusty. The only exercise you'll expend is crooking your trigger finger.

Elk are raised in pens for several reasons. Some are slaughtered, their meat sold to restaurants. Others are raised for their

antlers, which are collected when they are in the velvet and most potent as aphrodisiacs. Elk are also bred to develop superior genetics, and some are raised to be shot by shooter-clients.

Typically, owners of penned elk never use the word "pen" when they advertise. They refer to their operations as "game ranches", "elk ranches", or "preserves". Invariably, their ads will say their hunts are 100 percent guaranteed, no license is required, and there is no season. Of course, hunters will only be interested when bulls' antlers are hard and shed of velvet, normally from September to March or so.

The ads may also proclaim the Boone and Crockett (B&C) scores of the elk you can expect to shoot, proudly announcing the trophies that are waiting for you. The shoots are not cheap, ranging from $5,000 and up.

What the ads don't tell you is that their elk cannot qualify for the Boone and Crockett Club because the enclosure violates one of the B&C rules for fair chase. The B&C record book states it this way: "To make use of the following methods shall be deemed UNFAIR CHASE and unsportsmanlike, and any trophy obtained by use of such means is disqualified from entry: Hunting game confined by artificial barriers, including escape-proof fencing; or hunting game transplanted solely for the purpose of commercial shooting."

Smiley Arrowchis, a game warden on the Ute Indian Reservation, was one of Jim Zumbo's guides.

Billy Stockton, one of Zumbo's favorite outfitters, packs out an elk for a client. Outfitters perform a variety of services to make your hunt easier.

If the prestigious Boone and Crockett Club clearly states that hunting in an enclosure violates fair chase rules, can that be interpreted to mean that it's unfair to hunt in an enclosure? And if that's so, why do people persist in hunting in pens?

What we have here is an ethical consideration. Ethics are unwritten rules that are perceived differently by each individual. Every human has his or her set of values.

To some people, an elk is simply a species among many, having no special value. The notion of hunting an elk in its wild surroundings is not important, and may not even occur to those who hunt in pens.

I vividly recall my early elk hunting years. It took several seasons before I ever saw a decent bull, and by decent I mean something better than a spike. Granted, I was hunting a state that didn't have very many elk in those days, and I still remember the frustrations, as well as the sore legs and weary muscles. I became that much more determined to finally get it right and lay claim to my first bull.

From those early days to this, elk hunting has always meant a serious challenge, often ending in failure rather than success. To put this into a personal perspective, let me say that I hunt elk with a passion, pursuing them in three or four states each year. I come home empty from many of those hunts, because elk hunting simply doesn't lend itself to high success, especially on public land where I do a great deal of hunting.

What I'm saying is that an elk hunt means far more than shooting an elk. Though I live in the mountains outside Yellowstone Park and literally see elk 10 months out of the year from my window, I never tire of the quest when autumn rolls around and with it a new season. From the folks I talk to at seminars each year, my feelings aren't uncommon. To a real elk hunter, and by real I mean the man and woman who truly know what the pursuit is all about, it's simply okay to come home with an unpunched tag. That's elk hunting, and a very much accepted part of it.

That's why it's so difficult for me and other enthusiastic elk hunters to understand the mentality of those who are satisfied with shooting an elk in a pen. While I won't pass judgment on those individuals, I pity what they've missed. A tame elk in an enclosure is so far removed from his wild brethren that there's no comparison. Though the penned bull will bugle and carry out the breeding ritual, something vital is lacking, notably the wild component.

Most penned hunts are of one day duration, and shooters hardly get their boots dusty. Surely they don't complain of blistered feet, overworked lungs, or seeing too many grizzly bear tracks.

In all fairness, it's understandable why some people resort to game farms. I refer to those who are physically disabled or have a severe medical condition. That being said, there are hunts available in most states where wild elk can be pursued with a minimum of discomfort. I recall George Taulman, a New Mexico outfitter who, with a pair of guides, carried a hunter profoundly

disabled with MS to a ground blind overlooking a waterhole. The man was comfortably situated in his wheelchair, left on his own without a guide, and in a couple hours downed a fine bull. This was a bona fide wild elk hunt, with no confining fences.

Then there are those who suffer no such maladies, but find it quite acceptable to shoot a tame bull. Some of these individuals claim they don't have the time for a real elk hunt. I suspect that more than a few of those souls are in reality turned off by elk country and the rigors of the hunt. I know some who fear horses, bears, mountain lions, the forest, the dark, and other so-called perils of the elk woods, and there are some who loathe tent camps, outhouses, the absence of daily showers, and other inconveniences of the outback. In a nutshell, elk country and elk hunting isn't for everyone, thus we have a proliferation of penned hunts.

And what does the nonhunting public think about all this? In two words: not much. It's a documented fact that nonhunters are more prone to accept hunting if the participants use woods skills and work hard to find the quarry. A big turn-off to the nonhunter is the person who takes shortcuts, relies on modern technology, and hunts in an unsportsmanlike manner. It doesn't take a rocket scientist to understand that an animal in a pen is not terribly elusive, and that those who shoot those animals are taking the easy way out. Real hunters they aren't, and they make zero points with the folks who don't hunt. Worse, they make it a whole lot tougher for those of us who *do* hunt hard and within the parameters of fair chase. Another wedge is driven in the bona fide hunting scenario.

Some game farm operators will tell you their pen is big enough that a shooter is offered a true challenge. Hogwash. No pen can ever duplicate elk country and the serious challenges of a real hunt. If a challenge is really there, then why do game farm operators offer a 100 percent guaranteed hunt? Show me an outfitter who makes such boasts on unfenced lands and I'll show you a liar, or, at best, a person who hallucinates or has a serious drinking problem.

Other perils of game farms have been well documented, specifically the problems of disease spreading from tame elk to wild populations, and the danger of hybridization caused by animals that escape the fence. These two eventualities are not to be taken lightly. They are deadly serious matters. Consider the 2600 penned elk in Alberta that had to be killed because they carried tubercu-

losis, and the escaped penned elk and red deer that are still undestroyed and roaming wild lands in parts of the west.

Perhaps the best way to capsulize this issue is to quote an old veteran elk hunter I met 30 years ago. "You ain't huntin' elk unless it hurts," he said "You gotta feel pain." To that, let me add a comment. You gotta see the beauty of the elk woods, too, and experience all of it. You need to use your brain to outsmart your animal, and when you get blood on your hands, and beat yourself half to death moving several hundred pounds of meat out of the woods, you'll know what elk hunting is all about. That's something that the people in the pen will never understand. What a shame.

BUY IT FROM AN INDIAN TRIBE

Quite possibly the best elk hunts on the continent are held on Indian reservations, most of them in the Southwest. These hunts are also among the most expensive, running up to $12,000 or more.

Why so pricey? As they say, "you get what you pay for." On most reservations, what you get is a dandy, truly wild bull, probably bigger than any other bull you've ever taken. Some reservations, for example, offer bulls that *average* a B&C score of 350. That's huge in anybody's book, including Boone and Crockett.

So why do these reservations produce such enormous elk? There are three good reasons. Since most reservations are in the southwest, mild winters and quality feed translate to big antlers. Another factor is moderate hunting pressure. Hunters are limited, and low quotas mean more bulls to escape and grow older. Old bulls mean bigger bulls. Genetics round out the threesome. Many people, including me, believe that the Merriam subspecies did not go extinct around the turn of the century as some textbooks claim. One account states that the last Merriam was killed in 1904 on the White Mountain Indian Reservation in Arizona. It amazes me that in those days of little or no censusing techniques, someone could say the last elk was shot in a heavily timbered region that stretched unbroken for millions of acres. (Merriams were known for very large antlers.)

For whatever reason, you can be assured that you'll be treated to a fair-chase hunt with plenty of bulls running around. Most of the time, you'll be riding in a 4wd pickup, or perhaps some hiking. These are not generally strenuous hunts, though every situation is different. A bull that strikes your fancy on top of a ridge may

You Can Buy an Easy Elk   13

Elk are raised in pens for breeding purposes as well as their meat, antlers, and targets for hunters.

require everything you've got in the heart, lung, and muscle department to climb up to him if no roads are present. However, compared to elk hunts on public land where there's plenty of hunter pressure, I'd classify reservation hunts as easier hunts. Typically, tribes offer superb lodging accommodations, and food is outstanding.

Some reservations are so popular that a long waiting list is the norm. It may take several years before you're allowed to hunt. The bottom line, of course, is having the coins to afford a tribal hunt. If your Aunt Tillie passes on and leaves you a small fortune to play with, here's a good place to spend it if you're looking for the bull of your dreams.

I hunted on an Indian reservation just once. Here's the account of that hunt, as I described it in one of my hunting columns in OUTDOOR LIFE:

It was the kind of bull that an elk hunter's dreams are made of. The rack was enormous; massive, very wide with six long, symmetrical points to the side, each gleaming with bright ivory tips.

Neither Homey Sekacaku nor Smiley Arrowchis, my two full-blooded Indian guides, needed to offer a word of advice. All day we'd been evaluating bulls on the sprawling reservation, but I

required no help in sizing this one up. Instantly I placed the scope's crosshairs tight behind the elk's shoulder, drew a breath, and squeezed the trigger.

Homey Sekakuku, one of the Ute Tribal officials, was designated head chef for the hunt. His wonderful sense of humor kept everyone in high spirits.

But I'm getting ahead of myself. The hunt began years before, at least two decades of years, when I lived in Vernal, Utah. As a wildlife biologist for the federal government, I'd been well aware of the big bulls on the Ute Indian Reservation, which is just a few dozen miles from Vernal. In fact, every hunter in Utah was acutely aware of the elk as well, but the animals had been off limits to non-tribal members.

Even before that, in 1961, I hunted the reservation with college pals for deer. It was a big game mecca at the time, primarily for deer, and elk were just becoming established.

My early efforts at elk hunting the national forests around Vernal were marginally successful. I was just beginning to understand elk behavior, and made plenty of mistakes. It took several years before I saw a decent bull. Granted, Utah wasn't a premier elk state at the time, but I was nevertheless learning from the school of hard knocks.

As the elk herd on the Indian reservation grew, along with the stature of the bulls, I wondered what it would be like to hunt the big region. With more than one million acres within its borders, the Ute tribe was nurturing one of the finest elk herds in the nation.

I became acquainted with Homey at the time, and he told me tales of huge bulls that roamed the reservation. Homey's constant smile and sense of humor were contagious, and we joked about the day when non-Indians would be allowed to hunt the tribal land. Homey was an official with the tribal wildlife board and was genuinely interested in opening up the lands to hunting, but his efforts were unsuccessful.

I moved to Wyoming in the mid-1980s, leaving behind the northeast Utah area that would provide a lifetime of memories. My elk hunts took me all over the west and Canada, but I often reminisced about my Utah hunts. Every now and then something or someone jogged my memory of the Indian reservation, and I'd fantasize about hunting it all over again.

Homey and I were reacquainted in the summer of 1994 when I was giving seminars on elk hunting. With that same smile I'd remembered years ago, he shared with me the big news. The reservation would open to elk hunting in the fall, and he asked if I had any interest in participating. It was a foolish question.

A few months later, while driving out to hunting camp with Homey, I couldn't help feeling that I was regaining something that I'd lost years ago. The familiar cliffs, saltbrush flats and sagebrush valleys gave way to cedars, pinyon pines, and oakbrush patches that I hadn't seen for years. Finally we left the foothills and climbed into the higher elevations where we entered the reservation, and I could hardly contain my excitement, especially when the aspens came into view.

No forest captivates me as much as a gleaming, golden aspen stand in September. The essence of what the aspens stand for means as much as their natural beauty. When the foliage makes the annual transformation from green to the brilliant yellows and

oranges, elk bugling is in full swing. To me, nothing in the outdoor world is as enchanting as the autumn woods full of elk music.

Homey turned the vehicle into a side canyon and took us through a brightly lit aspen forest. The timber virtually glowed with light as the sun reflected off millions of leaves, and I wasn't a bit surprised when Homey slowed the truck to a halt and pointed to a bull elk feeding across the canyon.

By the time we drove into camp, we'd spotted a dozen more bulls, all branch-antlered animals, and none disturbed by hunters. It was destined to be a most interesting opening day, which began in the morning.

Camp was nestled in a draw, consisting of a series of cabins, and all within sight of elk that roamed the sidehills. There I met Bob Chapoose, Director of the Ute Hunting and Fishing Council, and his hunter, Tom Pallansch, who was as eager as I to open the season.

Homey fired up the barbecue grill, tossed on several huge steaks, and managed to cut his finger smartly as he was slicing onions. Given Homey's sense of humor and genuine humility, the rest of the evening was a series of laughs, though I wasn't distracted quite enough from thinking about the bulls that dwelled in the forests around us. That distraction was enormously enhanced later that night when I lay in my sleeping bag and listened to several bulls bugling nearby. How sweet it was.

My two guides had a tough time figuring where to begin the hunt on opening morning, since each had favorite spots. A decision was quickly made, and we headed for a ridge about six miles from camp. Arriving in the dark, we parked the truck and headed afoot to a vantage point atop a promontory.

Morning light revealed four bulls in the distance, feeding on a big plateau. They were too far for a good evaluation, so we moved in cautiously. At 300 yards we peeked and had a better look, but neither Smiley nor Homey were terribly impressed.

Suggesting that we could do much better, we headed back to the truck to try some other areas. Our initial plan that morning was to stay high and glass as many elk as possible. Later in the hunt, we'd head for more remote country if necessary.

Hunting a new area for big game always has its initial questions and doubts. Being unfamiliar with the area, you don't know exactly what it produces. What is considered to be a trophy in

other places might be far smaller, or larger, in the new place you're hunting. I know what a big bull looks like, but everything is relative. So it was that I depended on my guides for their input.

Later on that morning we spotted a good bull in a canyon. Though I was able to sneak within 150 yards, I couldn't get a clear look, though I judged he'd easily top the 300 B&C score, possibly scoring 325, which is good for any bull. The elk managed to slip away in the aspens with his cows, and being a herd bull, he wasn't interested in our bugle calls.

This was elk camp on the Ute Indian Reservation. Bulls could be heard bugling around camp all night long.

After hunting the rest of the day and looking at several mature bulls, we decided to make a long drive to a distant ridge that was Homey's favorite. As we traveled, huge thunderheads drifted across us, threatening a serious storm. Lightning flashed in the distance, and it appeared we'd be in for a deluge.

We were about to call it quits when we decided to check out a grassy flat off the side of the ridge. A deep-throated bugle from that spot sent us moving quickly, and as we eased over the ridge I spotted the giant bull I'd mentioned at the beginning of this story.

I needed no coaxing; a few moments later my Browning 7mm Mag cracked and claimed the bull at 200 yards.

In all my years of elk hunting, I'd never seen a prettier elk. The bull's fourth points were 22 and 21 inches long, and his long beams were heavy, each carrying six perfect points. Homey and Smiley were as impressed as I, and we admired the bull as lightning crackled nearby. Remarkably enough, a double rainbow appeared just as we finished field-dressing the elk, and ended just a few hundred yards away from us.

This was the first Indian reservation I'd ever hunted, and I may never hunt another. Several reservations in the southwest offer outstanding, but very expensive hunts for trophy bulls. A number of tribes are managing their elk herds for quality animals, and some reservations have a waiting list for permits. I considered myself truly fortunate to have had the opportunity to hunt one of the west's finest elk herds.

My elk rough-scored about 347, making it my best bull in three decades of hunting them. Though my elk hunts have taken me everywhere throughout the West and Canada, it was somehow fitting that my best bull came from the area I'd dreamed of most of my adult life. It was indeed a homecoming elk hunt.

BUY IT FROM AN OUTFITTER

In the major elk states, several thousand outfitters are available to take you hunting. They operate everywhere from pristine high country wilderness areas to lowland deserts, on private land and public land, and using all sorts of transportation methods, including horses, llamas, airplanes, boats, pickup trucks, ATVs, and the human foot.

The advantages of an outfitted hunt are numerous, but the major element is access. The outfitter simply transports you to an area you cannot reach yourself, either because it's off the beaten track and tucked into the boonies, or because it's private land that he owns or leases.

Once you've been delivered to the chosen spot with all your gear intact, you're then provided accommodations that should allow you to survive nicely, such as a warm and dry place to sleep (it may not be warm if the outside temperature is cold—more on that in the special chapter on outfitters), and nourishing food. After your human needs are considered, his next service is knowledge. He's responsible for taking you to the elk, helping you get within range, transporting the meat back to camp, and then finally to the trailhead or food processor at the end of the hunt.

For all these goodies, you can expect to pay anywhere from $2500 to $4500 or more. Prices are normally higher if you're headed to the backcountry on horseback, since an outfitter has a lot of money invested in hours and tack. It's not uncommon for an outfitter to own 50 to 80 horses. And, of course, he's got a sizable payroll, too, including cooks, wranglers, guides, and other help.

I'll explain all this in the chapter on outfitters, but let me say that the cost of an outfitter hunt doesn't include an elk. There are no guarantees; even the best outfitters operate less than 100 percent. So if you're considering buying an outfitted hunt, prepare yourself mentally to go home empty. Furthermore, an outfitted hunt may not be easy, either. More on that later.

Jim Zumbo took this New Mexico bull on a state wildlife area by drawing a lottery tag. Many public lands have outstanding elk hunting in these limited-entry units.

Chapter 3

You Can Win an Easy Elk

Of all the bull elk I've had the fortune of tying my tags to, one of the most memorable is a six pointer that I took in Colorado 10 years ago. He was far from being one of my biggest bulls, but I had a special satisfaction in taking him in a state where six-pointers are rare on accessible public land. I hunted U.S. Bureau of Land Management federal land, saw only two other hunters during three days of hunting, and the bull fell within 300 yards of a road. He was the 11th bull I'd seen on the hunt. That, folks, is quality hunting. It doesn't get much better than that.

On another bright note, the hunt wasn't expensive. Other than the nonresident fee, I bought gasoline, and that was all. I camped in my camp trailer on public land for free and ate home cooked food that I'd prepared and frozen before the hunt.

So how did I pull this off? Quite simple. I had accumulated enough preference points to guarantee me a tag in a limited entry unit that offered a small quota of elk tags with a very high hunter success rate.

Note the word *guarantee*. Lottery-drawn permits are supposed to be a gamble, where only a few lucky applicants are awarded tags. The key is the *preference* point.

Here's how it works: You apply for a tag, and if your name isn't drawn, you get your money back as well as a preference point. A computer in the Colorado Division of Wildlife office keeps track of your point. Incidentally, you may still buy a general tag over the counter and hunt during the regular firearms season in one of the many general units.

If you apply the following year and don't draw, you'll get a second preference point, and so on until you have enough to get a tag. Each limited entry unit has a different number of preference points that must be earned to get a tag. Obviously, the top units require the highest number of points. Right now, you'll need 10 to 12 points to win a tag in some of Colorado's very best units. That means a dozen years of applying, since you can get only one point per year. On the other hand, many decent units require far less points.

This big bull came from a ranch in southern Colorado that makes tags available to the public in a Ranching for Wildlife program. The tags are available in a lottery that allows preference points.

There is a profound down side of the preference point system. For example, I've now accumulated 9 preference points since I killed that bull 10 years ago. I'm a shoe-in for a tag next year, because that particular unit requires 9 points, and I'm a happy camper. However, a newcomer to the program who is just start-

ing to gather points may have to wait twenty years or more to draw my unit, and so will I once I start building points from scratch. Obviously, the hunter with plenty of points is sitting pretty, while the one with few or no points has a long road ahead. This is unfair to those "beginners", especially youngsters who are just coming of hunting age. My home state of Wyoming began a preference point system for moose and bighorn sheep three years ago. Because of the huge number of hunters applying for a limited number of licenses, you might wait a lifetime if you haven't gotten in when the program started. As one mathematics whiz told me, a youngster who is five or six now might be a grandparent before he or she is eligible to draw. Since minimum hunting age in Wyoming is 12, by the time the youngster is old enough, he or she will have a long wait.

Here's why it may take much longer if you're starting to earn points. Look at the preference point program as a pyramid having different levels. As you begin gathering points, you start at the broad base and work up to the top where you're then drawn. Each year, the base widens because more and more people apply. Because the tag quota usually remains the same, the pyramid also grows taller, requiring more time to reach the top.

This hunter won his bull tag in a Utah lottery. He took his chances and was awarded the highly prized tag.

A big herd of bulls on a limited-entry area near Mt. St. Helens in Washington. You can win a chance to hunt these elk by simply applying in the lottery.

Remember though, that each unit has a different number of qualifying points. Obviously, the best units are the most in demand, requiring the longest wait.

The bonus point system is another way to beat the odds, and operates in a completely different way than preference points. The system works like this: Let's say you apply for a tag, don't get it, but receive a bonus point. The following year, when you apply again, the bonus point becomes an extra application. Instead of one try at the tag, you have two. And so on. This is a much fairer system than preference points, because you can draw with no points the first year you apply. Obviously, multiple applications in the draw will greatly enhance your chances.

Bonus points may be free, or you may need to buy them. For example, Utah offers them at no charge, but you must purchase them in Nevada and Arizona. In Nevada, you send in the total fee for the tag, and you check off a box on the application indicating you want to buy a bonus point if you don't draw. If you're unsuccessful, the state will send you your money back, minus $101.00, which is the cost of the nonresident bonus tag. In Arizona, you must buy a nonresident $85.50 license before you apply for the tag. The state keeps the money and gives you a bonus point. Other states offer widely varying programs. In Washington, if you apply for a

limited entry area and don't draw, you get bonus points, but you forfeit the right to hunt the first three days of the general season.

Keep in mind that preference and bonus points may be available only for certain species, and some states allow you to accumulate only a limited number of points. In Colorado, for example, you can have no more than three preference points for bighorn sheep and mountain goats. If you intend to apply for those two species, you'll have at least a three year wait, and then there are no guarantees, since more and more hunters are accumulating their third point each year and are being added to the pool. Once you have the three points, your name then goes into a computer with everyone else having three points, and there is no longer a preference.

Despite the obvious advantage to the bonus and preference point systems, an amazing number of hunters ignore the possibilities. Each year I give big game hunting seminars at sportsmen's shows, and I ask my audiences how many of them are applying for points. Consistently, less than 10 percent try for tags, which always amazes me.

There are a few reasons why hunters don't apply. First, they believe they'll never draw because they aren't lucky, so they don't bother. The preference point system, of course, doesn't depend on luck, but perseverance. Second, the process to apply is often so complicated that people can't understand it. Third, when you draw a limited entry tag, that unit might be unfamiliar to you, and you can't hunt in your traditional spot.

None of those reasons hold much water if you really want to hunt a great area with a chance to take the animal of your dreams. Because limited entry units offer a quota of tags and hunter pressure is minimized, big game are allowed a better chance of survival, and will live longer. Age is directly responsible for antler quality in wild animals.

Recognizing this, practically every western state offers some kind of program. When considering a future hunt, think long term. Start building points now, and you won't regret it when that wonderful tag arrives in the mail.

There are a number of companies that will do all the applying for you. They'll keep track of your preference and bonus points, and will apply you in the best areas. This concept was originated by George Taulman, who owns United States Outfitters. Taulman

Merwin Martin drew a tag for an elk unit near Cody, Wyoming and killed this giant bull, which is among the top 10 in the world. The elk was taken on national forest land.

charges a one-time consultation fee for $100 per state and fronts the fee for elk, deer, and antelope applications. For example, say you're interested in applying for mule deer tags in Utah and Nevada. Taulman's company applies you indefinitely, or until you get the tag. He also pays the fee each year, as well as the cost of the bonus point (if any) which is billed to you at the end of the year. If you draw, you pay him the fee. (Taulman does not front fees for other big game such as sheep, moose, goat) The advantage of a system like this is obvious. Taulman's staff know the best units, they understand all the point systems, and they pay your fee until you draw. For information, contact United States Outfitters at 800-845-9929.

This chapter is the essence of this book. Limited entry areas are simply the very best places to hunt an easy elk, primarily on public land, and especially if you have an eye on the budget.

Chapter 4

Luck May Get You an Easy Elk

Most of us know lucky people who seem to beat the odds and have amazingly good luck, whether it's winning a church raffle item, a gun at an elk foundation banquet, or a quality elk tag offered in a lottery.

In this chapter I'm referring to the person who sort of stumbles on an elk, with not much forethought or effort. Ron Dube, a Wyoming outfitter buddy of mine, defines luck as the result of preparation meeting opportunity. Getting an elk can simply be a matter of being at the right place at the right time, whether you put any thought into it or not.

Here's an example of crazy luck that allowed a hunter to get his elk. He was involved in a card game with his pals, and the liquid refreshment was flowing quite well. Instead of hitting the sack early with his friends, he sat out by the fire by himself with a bottle of hooch and drank the rest of the night away.

His buddies found him passed out next to the fire when they arose at 4 a.m., and left him there when they went hunting. Our hero managed to sleep until 11 a.m., whereupon he made some coffee, poured a go-cup, and drove down the road. Sometime later he pulled over with a nasty hangover and fell asleep behind the wheel.

An hour later he woke up, shook the sleep out of his eyes, and took in the sights around him. He was parked off a Forest Service road, overlooking a ponderosa pine forest.

After hunting hard all week, Madonna Zumbo, author's wife, found this horseshoe on a ridge. It indeed proved to be lucky.

This hunter won a sweepstakes hunt with Jim Zumbo offered by Winchester Ammo. His luck allowed him a chance at this fine Montana bull.

Suddenly he saw movement, and made out a bull elk running almost directly toward him. He grabbed his rifle, jumped out of the truck, took aim at the bull which had stopped to stare at him, and shot the elk through the heart.

He dressed the elk, drove to camp, and found his pals eating lunch. They took a look at his bloody hands and assumed he was playing a joke. They hadn't seen nary an elk, and when they found he had actually killed a bull, they couldn't believe it.

Therein lies a popular saying: "It's better to be lucky than good." An easy elk may just be the result of good luck. Unfortunately, too many hunters anticipate luck, but it never happens to most. Elk typically need to be earned.

A couple years ago, my wife, Madonna had drawn a superb late season elk tag near our mountain home. We hiked up a half dozen canyons, up and over icy ridges, and through deep snow until we were physically exhausted. There was one day left to hunt, and, after we dragged in out of the woods, I called my neighbor and asked if he'd seen any elk around his place.

He replied that he'd indeed seen a dandy bull in his headlights as he drove home that evening just inside a national forest. The next morning we headed up the road, and, within several hundred yards of our house, spotted a very big bull. He charged down the mountain, I stopped him with my cow call, and Madonna made a great shot. I was able to drive to the elk.

In that case, luck had something to do with it, but we'd earned that animal fair and square. I still

This hunter won a tag in a sweepstakes hunt offered by the Rocky Mountain Elk Foundation. He hunted with Jim Zumbo (right) in Alberta, Canada, and took this huge bull.

After six days of hard hunting, this big bull strolled out into a meadow near camp where Jim Zumbo shot it. More than 45 hunters were camped in the area, and only one had gotten a bull all week. Zumbo was lucky.

Madonna Zumbo with huge bull she shot the day after finding the lucky horseshoe.

remember the pain and suffering as we withstood below-zero gales and climbed slippery steep slopes.

I can recall many other hunts where being in the right place at the right time resulted in meat on the table. But it's folly to take your chances with luck alone. You can help make luck happen by hunting smart, hunting hard, and learning everything you can about elk hunting. And remember, the biggest message in this book is to draw that lottery tag. If you don't try, you'll never give luck a chance. And in the case of preference points, it isn't luck at all—it's hanging in there long enough to get enough points to draw the tag.

Chapter 5

How Not to Get an Easy Elk

You can join the 80 out of 100 elk hunters each year who don't get an elk if you follow this advice. Of course, many of those hunters are unsuccessful because elk are—well—elk. I'm talking about the unfortunates who never get an elk, or maybe luck out and get one in a blue moon. Here's how to join that luckless fraternity. Incidentally, every year, while giving seminars on elk hunting, some people tell me that they've been elk hunting for 10 or 20 years and never shot an elk. I suspect that they follow some of the guidelines listed below.

First, make no attempt to learn about elk behavior. Hunt in total ignorance, expecting lightning to strike and your bull to show up just around the bend.

Don't get very far from your vehicle. Drive around a lot, especially in the daylight hours. Keep believing that every mile you put in will sooner or later end up with the reward of an elk crossing the road within rifle range. What the heck, luck may be in your favor.

Don't get out of the toasty sleeping bag until the sun is already making an appearance. After all, hunting season comes only once a year. This is the time to get out with the boys, enjoy a card game and a few beers until the wee hours of morning, and enjoy camp camaraderie.

Come in out of the woods long before dark. Shucks, you don't want to get lost out there, and you surely want to be in camp in time for happy hour.

Don't get in a habit of looking into open country for feeding elk in the daytime. They won't be there. Look for them very early in the morning and very late in the afternoon. During the day, hunt them in the timber.

If you're scouting or actively hunting and see absolutely no sign, hang in there for the duration of the hunt. It's too much trouble to try a new spot; besides, your third cousin hunted that very area five years ago and killed an elk there. It's just a matter of time before something shows up.

Find a clearing or meadow where elk have been feeding during the night and sit on it during daylight hours. Be sure you can see all the meadow, because an elk might show up any minute.

Go to camp for lunch and a nap. After all, elk aren't moving much in the daytime, and there's no sense disturbing the woods. Besides, those last few beers you had last night haven't exactly sat very well. Maybe you're a little hungover.

Drive your ATV down every trail you can find, especially those that are closed to ATVs. Hell, no one else has been down those trails on an ATV; maybe since you're the first, you'll see an elk. Besides, you've never seen a government ranger as long as you've hunted the area. You'll never get caught.

If you spot elk in a meadow just before dark, be sure to tell other hunters unfamiliar to you the good news. You want some respect from your peers, and they'll all know how good you are at spotting game.

Don't bother sighting your rifle in before you hunt. After all, it was right on last year, and you're sure it's fine, even though your brother-in-law borrowed it for a deer hunt two weeks ago.

Don't fret about replacing the worn tires on your pickup, and forget about fixing the jack that wasn't working very well a few months ago. If something goes wrong, someone else will come by sooner or later.

Assume that your pals will be handy if you shoot an elk. You've got your old pocket knife, and if you get a bull you can always come back for help. Hopefully your buddies will have tools and stuff.

Don't bother carrying a compass. You won't be going very far from a road, and besides, the sun is shining. You can always tell direction.

Forget the pesky daypack that holds survival gear such as matches, fire starter, space blanket, extra clothing, and stuff like that. You aren't planning on spending a night in the woods. That sort of gear is for other guys who don't know much about the outdoors. Hell, you've been hunting whitetails back east for 20 years. Just because this is your first western hunt doesn't mean you can't get along just fine.

One of the toughest aspects of elk hunting is moving the carcass. Be prepared and don't attempt this alone unless the hillside is very steep and you're in good shape. Even then, think twice.

Buy the best bugle call you can, and trust in it to produce when others won't. If a bull doesn't respond when you blow the call from the side of the road, assume no elk are within earshot. Keep driving down the road, blowing the call every few hundred yards.

Disregard a weather forecast that warns of an impending blizzard. You have a four-wheel-drive pickup, and even though your camp is at 9,000 feet, you can move it in a hurry if you have to. Besides, what do those weather guys know? They're usually wrong.

Forget about trying to get in shape before the hunt. You don't expect to get very far from the truck, anyway. Your elk is either gonna be easy, or to heck with it.

A good hunter never sees camp in the daylight. Stay in the woods all day. These hunters were on an outfitted hunt, and were relaxing the day after the hunt was over.

Chapter 6

Make Your Elk Hunt Easier

As you've read a number of times in this book, elk hunting isn't easy because of three major factors: steep slopes, vast unroaded country, and the necessity of moving a heavy carcass. It's possible to alleviate these physical endurance elements by hunting smart and taking advantage of terrain, existing roads, and a couple carcass transportation techniques.

It's popular for writers to advise elk hunters to get in shape before the season. That's great advice, and I'm guilty of writing it, but I've since come to understand that there are individuals who simply cannot get in shape any longer. I'm referring to elderly hunters, or those with physical handicaps, ranging from people with minor heart problems to those who can barely walk. I'm also referring to out-of-shape people who smoke heavily or are obese. I could say, "shame on you, get in shape," but I'll assume that you're reading this chapter because you aren't going to be in shape come next elk season, for whatever reason.

GET IT OUT EASIER

The first thing you need to do is figure out how to get your elk out. My best suggestion is to arrange for a local packer to bring your elk out on horses. The tab for this chore runs between $100 to $200, or more if the carcass is a long way in the boonies. While this might seem expensive, you'll quickly realize how cheap it is once you try to move the meat yourself, especially if a medical condition may make this a dangerous project.

Hunt in places where other hunters are about. Jim Zumbo is looking for a place to camp fairly close to a road where hunters are apt to drive bulls to him.

Most western towns have packers who will transport your elk. Chambers of Commerce as well as outfitter associations can supply you with contacts. It's wise to discuss a packing job before you go hunting to be sure the packer is available if you need his services.

If you can't find a packer, think wheels; nothing more, nothing less. It's far easier to roll something than to drag or carry it. Some hunters make their own, but commercial models are available. The best carrier I know has a single, sturdy wheel, handles on each end, and brakes. For information on this model, call 1-800-PAC ORSE.

If you *must* bone the carcass and carry it out in pieces, think lightweight. An average bull, minus the blood, bones, innards, bullet-torn and bloodshot meat, will yield around 200 to 250 pounds of meat. By carrying out only 40 or 50 pounds each trip, you'll be able to get it all out by making four to six trips. Depending on how far back the elk is, the terrain, and the amount of weight you can carry, you should be able to move everything in no more than two days.

HUNT SMART

The biggest obstacle you'll face on your elk hunt, other than getting the meat out, is finding a living, breathing elk. Unfortunately, that often translates to a nasty six-letter word: uphill. Take away the uphill, and your elk hunt suddenly becomes more user-friendly.

Here's how to eliminate uphill. In much of our elk country there are roads in valley bottoms and on ridges. Make a plan with your pals that will allow you to be dropped off on a ridge early in the morning, whereby you'll slowly mosey down the mountain, taking your time and all day to do it. Your pals will pick you up on the lower road that evening.

To do this, you must resist the temptation to explore places where you need to climb, and to avoid rockslides, blowdowns, and other obstacles. While this might affect your ability to thoroughly cover the mountain you're hunting, the objective here is to keep the pacemaker or newly installed heart valves merrily pulsing along. You'll be working with a handicap, but at least you aren't driving around or taking short walks from roads. You're actually penetrating elk country, and your chances of getting into elk are much better than taking the easier way out.

You don't need to suffer needlessly in bad weather. If a storm blows in, build yourself a warm fire and get comfortable. Be smart and safe.

Another possibility is to be a stander on a drive. Have your buddies drop you off where you can find a good vantage point, and wait and watch while they move through the timber, attempting to push elk to you and other standers. While elk can't be directed and go where they want to go, drivers create chaos in the woods, and animals sometimes run into standers at the perimeters of the drives.

Here's a trick that works reasonably well, but you need to forget everything I've written about getting back in remote country and leaving most other hunters behind. In this instance, you want to sit quietly where all sorts of people are in the woods. The idea is that they'll be pushing elk around, and with any luck, some animals will come your way. You don't need to be very far in the woods to do this. You can be dropped off on a secondary road and walk a few yards to where you can see well. Take your lunch with you and sit there all day. You'll have a far better chance of shooting your elk out where the action is than from camp.

That brings up a point. You can even shoot an elk from camp if you're patient and observant (and lucky). Some years ago, I took a middle-aged man on an elk hunt who won the hunt in a sweepstakes contest. This person admitted he'd had three open heart surgeries (he told me this after we'd ridden horseback seven miles to our drop camp), and was not interested in any serious exercise. He was from a large eastern city, and was so enthralled with Montana's high country that he really didn't care if he shot an elk or not. Just being there was enough.

I found a spot where he could sit all day and watch elk crossings no more than 300 yards from the tent. The man slowly walked to that point every morning, sat on a big log, and read a novel, glancing up every now and then to see what was going on. Over the course of five days he saw bull elk, bull moose, buck deer, and coyotes. He was as happy as a clam, even though he never made an attempt to shoulder his rifle.

In another chapter I thoroughly discuss drop camps. These are superb opportunities if you aren't in good physical condition, although you'll typically need to be able to ride a horse. The cost is far less than fully outfitted hunts.

Also in other chapters, I discuss other opportunities for the physically challenged, from hunting elk ranches to Indian Reservations to private lands, all of which will be more expensive than drop camps or public land hunts.

Jim Zumbo shot this Colorado bull by ambushing it near an old logging road. Many hunters in the area kept elk moving around.

Remember one important fact when you're out there. The sight of an elk may get the heart pounding big time. You may be tempted, in your efforts to catch up to an elusive elk, to run up hills, jump logs, dash across creeks, and otherwise behave in a health-threatening manner. Is an elk worth taking that risk? We always hear of people dying of heart attacks when shoveling snow around their houses. Other people come out of the elk woods with serious medical problems, and some come out in body bags. Hunt smart, and don't overdo it in the steep country where air is thinner and there are temptations to really hurt yourself.

TRY BOWHUNTING

Can bowhunting get you an easy elk? After all, bowhunters proudly claim that their challenge is the most difficult of all, saying their elk hunts are far more difficult than most because of the necessity of getting close to an animal.

I won't dispute that, but what I perceive to be the big challenge is the skill aspect rather than the physical one. The ability to shoot an arrow accurately is a must. Bowhunters have the luxury of hunting elk during the rut. In some states, they can start in August. Hunters often have a more willing quarry that is undisturbed by armies of hunters (as is the case during the firearms season). During bowseason, elk are not as elusive and wary, and are far more vulnerable. Because they're vocal, they're often easier to locate.

Wallows can be watched over from a treestand or ground blind, and waterholes can likewise be observed by a waiting hunter. These strategies can often be accomplished fairly close to a road.

So what we have is the first hunting season of the year, when elk haven't yet been chased around, and during a time when romance is in the air and bulls are not as cagey as normal. Hot temperatures coax elk to wallows and waterholes close to access points. Calling is an excellent option, and either-sex hunting is the norm; allowing cows to be hunted.

This is a superb time of the year to hunt elk, as tens of thousands of bowhunters will tell you. You can mosey around at your leisure, enjoying the autumn woods at its best. I won't go so far as to say that bowhunting is easy—it simply offers a more laid back option without the intense competition from other hunters. It's a quiet, relaxing time of the year when the elk woods are magic. That's plenty of reason to give it a try.

USE A MUZZLELOADER

Every year, more and more hunters are taking up with muzzleloaders. These blackpowder firearms offer only one shot, of course, and would seemingly be a far greater challenge than modern firearms. That being the case, then why would I suggest that they offer an easier hunt?

As with bowhunting, it's more a matter of timing, as well as special opportunities. Many states offer muzzleloader seasons that are before or after the general modern firearms seasons. The big deal here is the lighter hunting pressure. As I've said numerous times in this book, the fewer the hunters, the easier the hunting.

Some states have special units that are open only to archers and muzzleloader hunters, period. Some entire counties are open only to black powder hunting.

If you're intimidated by the uncertainty of firing the traditional guns, you can opt for in-line versions that are more reliable. Tony Knight, president of Modern Muzzleloading, Inc. made me a believer in the latter, and I've taken a half dozen elk with his guns.

Whether you intend on shooting a flintlock, percussion, or in-line, consider a blackpowder option the next time you're looking for an easier elk. While you must be more skillful at getting closer to your quarry as compared to a regular firearm, you might have many more opportunities. That in itself can translate to an easier elk.

Hire a local packer to bring your elk out. The cost will be nothing compared to the cost of an accident or injury you might suffer if you try this alone.

This bull has lost most of his velvet. His antlers will be hardened and cleaned off by late August.

Chapter 7

What Makes an Elk Tick?

The most successful elk hunters I know, and I mean folks who consistently get their animal year after year, are acutely aware of an elk's basic habits. There's absolutely no substitute for knowledge. If you know the behavioral patterns of your quarry, you'll have a far better chance of locating one.

This chapter will give you a detailed insight as to an elk's daily lifestyle pattern, starting in early fall, continuing through the rut, on into the transition or post-breeding period, and finally to the winter. Hunts are held during each of these four periods, and I'll explain the intricate relationships of elk that will give you a basic understanding of elk behavior. When you have a good comprehension of what makes an elk tick, you'll have a bit more of an advantage during your quest.

THE PRE-BREEDING SEASON

Some states allow bowhunting in August and early September. During this period, elk are beginning to prepare for the breeding period, (also known as the rut or bugle season) which normally occurs the last three weeks of September and the first week of October.

During the spring and summer, a bull's antlers grow at an amazing rate. In mid to late August, the velvet coating begins drying up and shredding. It falls off, and the bull helps remove it by rubbing his antlers on brush and saplings.

As members of the deer family, bulls shed their antlers each year. The antlers grow very rapidly, averaging a half-inch per day. This bull in velvet was photographed in June, by early August his antlers will be fully developed.

In the summer, mature bulls are quite gregarious and hang out in bachelor groups, quite content to live together in a herd. As the breeding season approaches, however, bulls go off on their own, looking for cows. Initially, bulls just sort of check out the pickings, and aren't quite serious about breeding. They'll bugle a bit, but their hearts really aren't into it.

As part of the ritual, they'll visit a wallow, almost on a daily basis, and roll in the mud just as a pig would. The bull urinates on his belly, brisket, and neck while wallowing, and also urinates in and around the wallow. He thrashes nearby shrubs and trees with his antlers, rubbing so hard that the bark peels off, leaving a glistening yellow scar that can be easily spotted by hunters and other elk alike. Some biologists believe the wallow is a territory marker, used exclusively by individual bulls.

THE BREEDING SEASON

This is the marvelous period that appeals to those who love elk and elk country. Picture yourself being out there on a chilly morning, when quaking aspens are a riot of shining yellow, gold, and orange, and when frost glistens from lovely meadows, betraying

the route of every animal that disturbs the jeweled glaze coating every leaf and blade of grass.

Now imagine the spine-chilling sound of an elk's bugle call, echoing about in the sweet smelling breezes of the western mountains. This is the quintessence of autumn, a period of time that every serious big game hunter should experience at least once.

During this time, from early September to early October, mature bulls are dead serious about breeding. They locate herds of cows, driving out yearling bulls that often hang out with cows and calves, and defend their harems against other challengers.

Bugling is a constant activity during this period, and is performed for a variety of reasons. Bulls bugle to warn other bulls to stay away, they bugle to assert their dominance, and they bugle to reassure their cows.

There is a great deal of movement among cows during this time, especially when herds are active in late afternoon, through the night, and during early morning hours. Individual cows or small groups of cows and calves may wander away, regardless of the bull's antics or pleading calls.

Because much of the bull's activity is determined by the cows, bugling is at its peak during those hours of cow movement. This is the chief reason you'll hear more bugling early in the morning and throughout the night. Most observers recognize that fact, but I've never yet read this explanation. It makes sense.

During the rut, elk rub their antlers on trees as part of a breeding ritual. This is not done to remove the velvet covering, but as a display to advertise to other elk.

Bugling is also much more active when a cow is in estrus (heat). Other bulls scent the receptive cow, and move close to the group. The herd bull remains busy chasing off other bulls, and, in fact, his romantic cow is often bred by a young bull who slips into the herd when the harem master is busy chasing away another intruder. I've witnessed cows being bred by an interloper a half dozen times.

Herd bulls will collect as many cows as he can. I've seen harems ranging from a single cow to as many as 86. The average is anywhere from eight to fifteen or so.

Remember that calves are mixed with cows, remaining with them throughout the breeding season. There is a great deal of vocalization going on between cows and calves, especially when the herd is feeding or moving about. There is little or no vocalizing when the animals are bedded during daylight hours.

Herd bulls often don't retain their dominance of the harem for very long. A more aggressive bull might come by and steal the cows by out-bluffing or actually fighting, though the latter is rare.

Cow elk will determine the habits and behavior patterns of bulls during the breeding season.

When there's a confrontation between a herd bull and challenger, the scenario usually goes like this: the intruder bugles his intentions, moving closer toward the herd. The herd bull bugles

back, rushing out to meet the opponent. The two bulls run toward each other, but stop when they're five to 25 yards or so apart. Each bull will thrash a nearby sapling, usually bugling in the process. By some intimidation factor that we humans haven't yet figured out, one of the bulls will turn and run. The victor is the one doing the chasing, but he never really catches up, just going through the motions of being the tough guy.

Bulls may fight viciously during the breeding season to win cows, or they may spar in a more friendly fashion after the rut is over.

The parallel march is another form of confrontation. Each bull runs alongside the other, maintaining a space of two or three yards apart. This might continue for several hundred yards, until one of the bulls breaks the pace and runs off, or when one of the bulls actually lowers his antlers and charges. The other bull will meet the charge or run off.

When antler contact occurs, the fight becomes a pushing and shoving match. The loser normally is the one who is being pushed backward the most, and eventually he retreats with the victor in hot pursuit. Occasionally a bull will suffer a serious or even a fatal wound from a tine puncture during the battle, but often only their pride is hurt.

In most cases, the more aggressive bull is the winner, whether the confrontation is a bluffing game or a real fight. He is a master of intimidation, coming across as being mean and ornery.

Notice I said a more *aggressive* bull than a *bigger* bull. What does the word *bigger* mean in the world of elk? Do you suppose an elk judges an adversary by the number of points he wears, or the mass and length of his opponent's main beams and tines?

I think not. A bull has no idea what he wears on top of his head. He has no way to tell if his rack is more prominent than that of an adversary. It's the temperament of the challenging bull that means everything, provided we're matching bulls of about the same body size and age class. I've seen a modest five-point bull with fire in his eyes charge angrily into a herd, while the much larger six-point harem master ran off, totally intimidated by the smaller bull.

Generally, the oldest bulls have the most massive antlers, and they're often the most aggressive. But it isn't necessarily true that the largest bulls end up with herds of cows, or even the biggest herds of cows.

No matter how hard he tries, a herd bull may not be able to keep his cows in his harem. Some may simply walk away.

POST-BREEDING SEASON

When cows are no longer in heat, the yearly romance is over. This usually occurs in early to mid October, though there are exceptions.

Bulls will often stay with herds of cows or they'll live solo. Because most general hunting seasons begin after the rut, hunt-

ing pressure forces elk to stay in the timber longer than usual, coming out only in the evening to feed in grassy meadows and clearcuts.

A hunter checks out a huge rub made by a bull in Montana. Rubs often mark a bull's territory. Pay attention if you see many rubs, even long after the rut. The bull may still be around.

During this period, vocalization among bulls ceases, but cows and calves continue their chatter. If you were to blow a bugle this time of year, you'd be wasting your time, but there are exceptions, depending on when you were hunting. If it's mid-October, you might arouse a bull who believes you're consorting with a cow in heat. He's not apt to approach, but at least you can locate him and move in his direction, using the bugle call or cow call or both.

Since bulls no longer keep harems, groups of cows tend to bunch together in larger groups as fall progresses. Bulls also join up together, forming herds of two to ten or more.

Bulls lose a great deal of weight during the breeding season. Survival is a priority, since they must regain plenty of pounds before winter sets in. They feed extensively during the post-breeding period, but not to the point where they'll endanger themselves. Practically all their feeding occurs at night if they seek open meadows, or they'll remain in the timber if enough grass is available.

LATE SEASON

During most years, mid-November is the start of winter. Heavy snows blanket the high country, requiring elk to paw through snow to reach food beneath it. Elk begin migrating at this time, moving to lower elevations, often following well-established routes. Winter ranges are often located in valleys, riverbottom areas, ranches and farmlands, and other places that have light snow cover.

In some regions, elk remain on high, windswept ridges where the constant wind blows snow away, leaving grass exposed.

Late hunts are often the finest for someone who wants a big bull, especially where elk migrate out of refuges such as national parks and onto areas where hunting is allowed.

By this time, mature bulls are grouped in bull herds, and cows, calves and younger bulls gather in very large herds numbering 100 or more.

On the famous National Elk Refuge in Jackson, Wyoming, an average of 8,000 elk migrate in each fall and spend several months eating hay. As the snow recedes in the spring, they begin a reverse migration, slowly working their way back to summer ranges in higher elevations. This is the typical pattern of elk everywhere that migrations occur.

My wife, Madonna learned first hand how effective late season hunting can be. Read more about it in another chapter.

CHAPTER 8

ELK COUNTRY ISN'T USER FRIENDLY

Elk are animals of the north. Scientists tell us they came to North America from Siberia around 10,000 years ago during the Ice Age by walking across the Aleutian Islands. At that time, the islands were not islands, but a long strip of land and ice.

The new residents of North America settled into different habitats, and evolved accordingly. Six different subspecies roamed much of the continent, most of it in cold country with four established climatic seasons (two of those subspecies, the eastern and Merriam, are now extinct). Some of that country is milder than others, such as the California region inhabited by the Tule elk. It's quite dissimilar from the area that is home to Canada's Manitoba elk, or the high country of the Rocky Mountain elk.

The Roosevelt elk of the west coast, chiefly in Oregon and Washington, lives in unquestionably the most difficult habitat. Much of it is rain forest, where you practically have to crawl through holes in the wet brush, or along slimy logs laying crisscross above the forest floor.

Many years ago, when I was studying forestry in college, I took a summer job cruising timber in western Oregon. The undergrowth was so dense my partner and I had to wear head lamps on our hard-hats to see each other in the daytime at distances of less than 10 feet. This country defies all imagination. You cannot begin to comprehend how bad it is until you've tried to penetrate it. Not

only do trees grow tightly together, but the dense underbrush would almost repel a snake. Ferns, thorny bushes called Devil's Club, brambles, and other nasty bits of foliage grow tightly woven, offering a curtain that prison security designers might take a look at. Add to all this a lot of water, and I mean a lot of water, in the form of rain, fog, and drizzle, and you have one of the toughest chunks of elk country on the planet. This is definitely not the place to go if you want an easy elk.

This is typical elk country. It's steep, heavily timbered, and unroaded. This is one of the primary reasons why elk hunting isn't easy.

You'd think that resident hunters would dive into this stuff and claim an elk every year. Not true. A few locals hunt the thick jungle, but most are content to look for elk from log landings, which are vehicle-accessible places where loggers gathered and loaded logs. The strategy here is to glass the clearcuts from a pickup truck via binoculars or spotting scope, and then make a stalk, hopefully where the going is easy. Unfortunately, the going is often as tough in clearcuts as in the timber, what with logging debris and heavy undergrowth that carpets the old logged areas.

Other strategies, where roads are closed with locked gates, are to simply park at the gates and walk down the roads, hoping to see a dumb elk that is exposed outside the protection of the forest.

For those few who do hunt the jungles—they have my deepest respect. I admire their tenacity and dedication. These people, in my opinion, are truly the most enthusiastic elk hunters I've ever met. It's true that there are plenty of tough hunters in the Rockies, but even that mountain range cannot compare to the west coast rain forests.

Tule elk, a subspecies that lives in California, have been hunted for the last several years, and are truly easy elk since they live in open country much of the time, though pockets of brush and forests may conceal them in some areas. The tough part of hunting the Tule elk is getting a tag. Comparatively few tags are offered; all of them in a lottery, though a few are auctioned off. As expected, they cost a small fortune in the better areas.

In the Rockies, elk live everywhere from sagebrush deserts to pinion pine- cedar forests, to aspens, lodgepole pines, firs, and up into the alpine country. Generally speaking, elk in the lower sagebrush and cedar country are seldom hunted during a general season because they're more vulnerable. In the lower elevations they're more easily located, and vehicle access is often extensive. For that reason, those elk almost always are hunted by people who draw tags in a lottery.

Trying to find elk—and get to them—in this vast country may be a tough chore.

Jim Zumbo carries his camp up a steep mountain to elude other hunters. Very few will penetrate deep into this mountainous area.

By and large, most elk are in the mid to upper elevations. They're quite at home in the densest timber they can find. Show me a spruce-fir blowdown on a steep slope, and I'll show you fresh elk droppings.

Elk like being cool, and tolerate extreme cold. The only reason they migrate is to find adequate food in the lower elevations. In the winter, the higher reaches are blanketed by several feet of snow. Elk leave because they must, but will often linger on a high windswept ridge where consistent winds blow the snow away. If plenty of grass is available, they'll stay there all winter.

Besides timber, other obstacles that make elk hunting tough are very steep slopes. Elk have no problem negotiating mountainsides, although they like to cross a ridge through a saddle, which is a low spot. Rockslides are commonly traversed by elk; some of which require everything a human has to get through them.

In very high country, air will be thin, causing even more problems. This is especially true in Colorado, where elevations of 9,000 feet are commonly hunted. To a lesser degree, this is also true of other central Rocky Mountain states. I've hunted elk at almost 12,000 feet in Colorado. I can assure you that your body doesn't want to work very well that high, and everything you do must be in slow motion.

Elk are also showing up in the midwest, east, and south, thanks to efforts by state wildlife agencies and the Rocky Mountain Elk

Foundation. As I write this, elk will be hunted for the first time ever in Arkansas this fall. There are also growing herds in many other states. Elk country in these areas is basically hardwood forest, though in some places there are pine and spruce forests as well. Elk tend to remain in the same areas, and typically aren't tough to locate. As a result, hunting success is usually very high.

Studies show that in the western mountains, very few hunters travel much more than half a mile from a road. There are three reasons for this, two of which are directly related to elk country.

The first is because hunters are too unwilling to tackle the steep slopes, either because they're basically lazy, out of shape, or physically unable to meet the challenge. The second reason is the fear of getting lost. For the most part, elk country is vast, much of it unroaded. When the sun isn't shining, hunters are easily confused. As far as that goes, some hunters are confused even when the sun *is* shining. The third reason is because of the need to move a very large dead animal through that rough country. Hunters use their heads and don't travel farther than their ability to transport an animal out.

Elk country has many faces. This aspen forest is well used by elk. Notice how they ate the bark from the trees.

If you haven't tackled elk country yet, don't assume everything will be peachy fine. Get in the best physical condition you can; of course, under your doctor's supervision. Notice I said to get in the best shape

you can. Everything is relative in life; some of us ain't going to get in great shape any more, because of a certainty called old age.

Another chapter tells how to make it easier on yourself if you aren't in good condition. Heed the advice.

Elk country can be unforgiving when the weather turns bad. But this is the time when elk hunting is often as its very best, and Jim Zumbo sticks with it.

Chapter 9

The Easiest Elk of All

If you want to be successful on your elk hunt and aren't hung up on antlers but would welcome some tasty meat, consider taking a cow elk. Tags are fairly easy to get; in fact, both Wyoming and Utah recently allowed hunters to take a second elk as long as it's antlerless. This is an unprecedented move, indicating that many elk herds are doing so well that their numbers need to be thinned.

Few hunters consider cow elk when they think of elk hunting. In reality, most elk states require large numbers of cows to be harvested to keep populations at the carrying capacity of the habitat.

There are some interesting myths about the role of cows in the breeding scenario. A primary one is the cow's attraction to a particular bull, generally one who has superior antlers. As the story goes, the cow selects the bull she wants, forsaking all others.

I say hogwash; and wonder if some biologists and college professors who write that stuff ever get out of their air-conditioned offices to see what's really going on in the elk woods. My observations, along with those of others who have watched elk intently, strongly reject this possibility. Cows are bullied by a dominant, aggressive bull, pure and simple. She and her calf and other herdmates have no choice. When a bull wants his cows to move, he moves them by making threatening gestures with his antlers and quick forward steps. If the cow doesn't move, which is rare, he runs at her rapidly with his antlers tilted to the side, and she moves—quickly.

The notion of cows selecting a bull is simply not the case. Some cows have a stubborn streak and will merely walk away from the harem master, no matter what he does, and how huge his antlers are.

Here's a typical scenario of a cow not choosing the dominant bull. I watched a very big bull working himself to a frenzy running off smaller bulls. He had seven cows, and one was obviously in heat because he wouldn't leave her alone. He seemed so tired he couldn't mount her, but made half-hearted attempts. At one point, three raghorns moved dangerously close, approaching the herd master and his cows. The big bull took after two of the raghorns, and while the big guy was off in the woods tearing after the intruders, another little bull swiftly ran up to the cow, mounted her, and, with a wham, bam, thank you, ma'am, got the job done. She stood for him, and made no effort to move away. By the time the big bull returned, the little guy was gone, and the herd boss never had a clue that his lady was unfaithful. This is just one example, I've seen it happen dozens of times.

Another myth is that a herd always keeps a cow posted as a sentry, watching for danger while the group feeds. That's not so, either. Cows are always looking for danger, more so than bulls. Their maternal instincts compel them to watch out for enemies, because they've done so since they had their first calf. A bull has only to watch out for himself. He's done so since he was born, because he had to protect nothing but his own hide.

This is not to say that bulls are dumb compared to cows—they're simply not as sharply tuned to the environment. That's why you'll often see one or two cows looking about when the rest of the herd is feeding. It's their nature. If you watch long enough, every cow in the bunch will glance around now and then.

Cows are pretty complacent critters. During the heat of the bugle season, they seem completely disinterested in the antics of the bull. They mosey around, feeding calmly, and are controlled only by the herd bull's aggressiveness. Only when each cow comes in heat will she become interested in the bull. She will stand still and allow the bull to mount and breed her. The whole process takes less than five seconds. That's about all the interest she ever has in the bull-five seconds a year!

When a cow is close to being in heat, the bull is constantly near her, often getting her up from her bed by brandishing his antlers,

and basically harassing her until she finally allows him to mate her, but only when she's fully in heat.

In areas where herds are numerous, a cow will often simply take off and leave to join another herd. Often a bull cannot turn a truly stubborn cow, no matter how frantic his actions.

Cow elk make up the biggest part of the elk population, and are the easiest to find.

Once, I watched a cow leave a huge herd bull who had 81 cows and calves in his harem. She simply took off and walked across a river while he bugled and whined and basically made a fool of himself. He followed her halfway across the river, bugling and pleading, but she wouldn't return.

Sometimes a cow or a small group will bolt and run, leaving the herd bull frustrated as he tries to chase them down.

According to some new research, there's a bit of trading that goes on during the night. Cows leave herd bulls, and head for other herds or just wander about. I believe this is the primary reason that bugling is much more frequent during the early morning hours. After an evening of activity, with cows moving off and splitting from herds, the harem master runs about feverishly, trying to regain control and regroup his ladies.

Cow elk are extremely gregarious. You'll seldom find one alone, unless she's been temporarily split from the herd by hunting pressure or is having her calf.

In May or June, each pregnant cow takes off for a secluded area where she gives birth to a single calf. Twinning is extremely rare. Shortly after the calf is born, the cow rejoins the herd. She hides her calf as she feeds, returning to it when it's ready to nurse.

The calf makes a high-pitched chirp, which is nicely imitated by the standard cow call. When stressed or in danger, the calf makes several squalls. This type of vocalization continues into the fall months during hunting season.

Mimicking a distressed calf has obvious advantages, no matter when you try it in the fall. An inquisitive cow who hears your calls may come looking, and bring the whole curious herd with her, including the bull.

The cow also makes the chirp, and it can be of different pitches. I believe the basic difference between the cow and calf vocalization is the frequency and duration. The calf seems to call more often, with longer chirps, though it's easy to be confused. I don't think it's possible to precisely define each call, because they're so similar.

Merely using the cow call has so many logical implications that any hunter who doesn't use it is really missing out on an important tool.

It's necessary to blow the call softly if you're trying to imitate a cow. A loud call will more likely imitate a squalling calf. Don't blow the call repeatedly; wait 10 seconds between each soft mew, and vary the pitch as well. Blow the call three or four times, and then wait several minutes.

Cows and calves vocalize when they're active, seldom when they're bedded. You'll get more response in early morning and late afternoon hours.

By using the call when you're merely walking through the woods, you'll put any elk within earshot at ease. They'll think you're other elk, and will allow you to get closer than usual. They'll have you pinpointed, however, and at some point will figure out the betrayal, but at least you'll approach much more closely.

Once they've realized you're danger, elk will bust out in a great deal of noise and dust. That's where the cow call will stop them in their tracks. Simply blow on the call as loudly as you can. I believe this sounds somewhat like the bark of a spooked cow. If you've

ever seen a cow bark, you'll note that the other elk stop what they're doing and look at her. They take off only when it's been determined that there is a real threat.

You can stop running elk by using this sharp call even if they've seen you. In fact, it also works if you've shot and missed them. I've also seen it work when the elk is actually hit.

Many states offer cow tags because elk numbers must be adjusted to meet the carrying capacity of the land they live on.

This sounds far-fetched, but it works. Somehow the elk become so curious that they just can't stand it. They have to stop and look. Once, I was hunting in a snowstorm and a bunch of elk were crossing a big sagebrush patch in front of me. I blew my cow call sharply, and every elk stopped and looked. I took the only bull in the bunch, a five-point. I never would have fired if I hadn't stopped them because they were 300 yards away and running. Ain't no way I'm ever going to shoot at anything running 300 yards away.

My daughter Judi once drew a bead on a running bull and missed it. I blew on the cow call, and unbelievably, the elk stopped. She shot and missed again, and I stopped him again. This happened two more times until she managed to hit him squarely. Her scope was off because it had been bumped when we were riding horseback that morning, and if I hadn't blown the call, the bull would have been history.

I couldn't believe the bull stopped every time I blew the call, even though he was being shot at. It was an amazing incident.

Another option of using the cow call is to calm animals that you've spooked and actually call them back if the herd has been separated. The first time I tried this was in eastern Oregon. I jumped several dozen cows and they split up into two groups. I waited until the woods settled down, and softly blew the cow call. Nothing happened. I blew it again, and got an answer from a cow. Suddenly, a cow from the splintered herd responded, too. Soon, I was talking to both herds. A while later, I saw movement in the forest, and here came a bunch of cows headed my way. I had a bull tag, and didn't see one. Then I spotted the other bunch; there was no bull with them, either. More importantly I realized what happened. After being busted up, the animals were trying to regroup. They locate each other by calling, and I fooled them into believing I was part of their group.

You may see cows fairly close to roads, but finding bulls may be another story.

Most of the cows I've shot were taken in late season when they're closer to roads. Around November, animals are usually in much bigger herds, and drift to lower elevations where they'll spend the winter.

Don't be concerned, by the way, if you've shot a cow and she's "wet", meaning she had a calf at her side. By early fall, calves are weaned, and do well by themselves. And the social structure of elk is such that loner calves will immediately be accepted back into the herd.

And don't underestimate the culinary delights of cow elk meat on your plate. There's nothing better in the woods.

CHAPTER 10

THE EASIEST BULL OF ALL

The bull elk challenged me when I bugled toward the forested basin. I sat quietly in the little clump of trees I'd selected for a stand, and waited for him to make the next move. When he remained silent for five more minutes, I blew into the mouth call again. The elk answered immediately, and this time he was much closer.

A few moments later I spotted movement in the thick spruces. I glassed the area with my binoculars and saw the sight I had hoped for. A cream-colored animal with chocolate mane was slowly moving toward me.

I flipped off the safety, rested my .30/06 solidly on a branch, and found the elk in the scope. I nudged the cross-hairs toward his head and found what I was looking for. It was a bull.

This time the crosshairs found the chest area where his lungs were working. When I squeezed the trigger, the elk dashed wildly into the timber, but I knew he was mine. I walked over and found him dead about 10 yards from where he had stood when I fired. It was a fine spike bull.

This is the scenario that occurs tens of thousands of times each year. But this interesting aspect of elk hunting is unknown to hunters who don't live in elk country, perhaps because all they know about the subject is what they read in outdoor magazines. Outdoor writers generally relate stories only of lovely bulls, magnificent five-and six-point animals that weight upwards of half a ton.

What most outdoor writers don't tell you is that fewer than 10 percent of the elk killed in the United States are mature trophy bulls. The rest are cows, calves, "rag horns" (small three- or four-pointers), and spikes. Of all the bulls killed in the country each year, 50 to 70 percent are spikes.

This is a typical spike bull, with single unbranched antlers about 18 inches long.

Westerners and nonwesterners who hunt elk a great deal will generally kill the first spike that walks by. Why? Because they know the chances of seeing a big bull are slim in most regions. In most hunting circles, any bull is a good bull. Furthermore, a spike bull is perhaps the best eating of any big game animal. His flesh is so similar to grain-fed beef that I take pleasure in fooling

friends who would never knowingly eat deer or elk meat. I never tell them afterward that they've eaten part of a spike elk, either. Ignorance is bliss.

To be sure, a spike bull has none of the sagacity and caution of an adult bull who has avoided hunters for three or more years. The yearling bull is unwise to the ways of man and quite vulnerable to hunters. Because spikes usually remain with their family unit through their second winter, they use the old cows as protectors. No doubt their dependence on mama keeps many of them out of trouble and alive. Cows are the eyes and ears of the herd and are the leaders when danger threatens. Indeed, an old cow leads the herds during migrations as well as in escape from enemies. The big bull is usually the last in line.

When breeding season arrives, spike bulls are seen as competitors in the herd by big bulls. Though they've been part of a family unit with cows and calves since they were born, now they must leave temporarily. Mature bulls chase them out of the herds, but spikes often run off a short distance and keep just far enough away to keep the herd bull happy. Spikes are sexually mature, and some observers feel they actually do much of the breeding when the herd bull is off challenging a competitor. Then the spike moves in quickly and breeds a cow.

When a spike is split off from the rest of the herd, he is suddenly on his own. In September when most young bulls are driven from the cows, they are about 18 to 20 months old. This is the time bugling season occurs, and spikes will respond to a call made by a hunter. This is not to say a spike bull is a foolish animal. He lacks the instincts of older bulls but has learned much from his mother. Any careless move on the part of the hunter will put a spike to flight instantly.

Almost every bull elk begins his adulthood as a spike, although a few young bulls have forks on one or both sides while others have three or four small points. But it's safe to say that the single spikes are the starting antlers for 90 percent of the bulls that are yearlings.

The term spike is a bit misleading, because the antler isn't straight but curved. Studies of thousands of spikes indicate the antlers can be anywhere from 10 to 24 inches long. Generally, the spike antler retains its velvet sheath until the antler drops off in late winter or early spring.

On occasion spike bulls will be allowed to remain in the harem of cows by the big herd bull, perhaps because the larger bull sees the spikes as no threat.

Spike bulls are more numerous than mature bulls for obvious reasons. During its first autumn, the male elk is a calf without antlers, and its chances of surviving the first hunting season are excellent.

A few hunters take calves during antlerless or either-sex seasons, but most settle for a big dry cow. The next year, those surviving males with their new antlers are suddenly legal quarry in areas that allow any bulls to be harvested. Thus, a new generation of bulls are available to hunters.

Many states have enacted regulations protecting spikes in an effort to produce older bulls in the herds. By allowing spikes to survive, they'll be mature the following season. Conversely, some states now allow *only* spikes to be taken in many units. This is designed to protect older bulls. In some areas, mature bulls in those spike-only units can be hunted if you draw a special lottery tag.

Since spike bulls hang out with cows and calves whenever they can, they're more vulnerable to hunters, simply because it's easier for hunters to locate an elk herd than a lone bull. Tracks are easier to find and follow, a herd is more visible, and a group of elk often makes plenty of noise. Cows and calves normally squeal and bark at each other when feeding or traveling leisurely through the woods.

Once, when I was hunting elk in Montana, I heard the telltale noises of an elk herd across the canyon I was watching. I glassed the timber and saw a group of elk moving from the trees into a long meadow. No herd bull was present, but two spikes were in the midst of the cows and calves. I left my vantage point, made a stalk across to the elk, and killed a fat spike with 20-inch-long antlers. I might not have seen the elk at all were it not for the noises they made, since I had intended to leave the area about the same time I heard them.

If the wind is right and the woods are reasonably quiet, it's possible to stalk into shooting range of a herd of bedded elk. If it's breeding time, the herd bull might be right in with the cows and calves; otherwise a spike could be in the vicinity.

In areas that are heavily hunted and cover is sparse, opening-day hunters get the pick of the elk and quickly harvest the spikes.

This is a good reason to be ready for the opener unless your heart is set on a mature bull. But if it's a "meat" bull you want, locate the elk herd as fast as you can and pick out the spike, if one is available.

A big spike will weigh upwards of 350 - 400 pounds, and is as tasty-eating as any animal you'll ever hunt.

In the event that you're hunting in the snow, tracks are obvious and you have the advantage of determining how fresh they are. Mixed with other elk tracks, a spike bull's print isn't easily identified. Small cows and big calves could be mistaken for a spike's track. But if you spot a set of medium-sized tracks by themselves, chances are good that you're looking at prints made by a spike. Cows seldom travel alone, since they're accompanied by calves or other cows. If a big bull is traveling alone, you can tell by the size of his track. But a loner spike can often be identified by his tracks because other elk seldom travel alone, at least elk that own feet the size that a spike bull does.

During bugling season, a lone spike might answer a call out of curiosity. He won't be looking for a fight, but he'll be interested in the new bull in the territory. Spikes don't bugle with the same intensity and pitch that a mature bull does. At best they cut loose with a high-pitched squeal.

Bow hunters often get a good crack at spikes because bow seasons are often earlier than rifle seasons, and spikes have just been kicked out of the herds by bigger bulls. A friend of mine takes a spike bull almost every year with an arrow by capitalizing on that knowledge. He lures lonely spikes into bow range by bugling in areas where several herds traditionally live.

Generally speaking, cows, calves, and spikes often inhabit lower elevations than adult bulls do. This is not a rule but a personal observation. That means foothill areas blanketed with pinyons, junipers, and pockets of quaking aspens. The bigger bulls will be in the rough lodgepole pine and alpine fir timber farther up the mountain. Spike bulls won't necessarily be easy to find and kill, but at least they'll be more available.

Though he's a yearling, a spike bull will weigh 250 to 400 pounds fielddressed. A suitable firearm is one that will anchor a big mule deer or whitetail, but the elk hunter never knows if he's going to send a bullet into a spike or his granddaddy.

The spike bull will never be a celebrity in the woods, and few writers will write about him. But he's present everywhere there are elk, and though few hunters will grace the wall with his head, he's not to be looked down upon. The trophy hunter will pass him up, hardly giving him a second glance, but to the great majority of hunters, the spike is an honorable quarry, a "meat bull." He's not the Bull of the Woods, but he's still bigger than any mule deer or whitetail you've ever shot. Unless I'm after a trophy, I'll draw down on a spike whenever I can, and so will most other elk hunters. He's a fine game animal, one to be respected. And don't be surprised if you kill a spike bull and smile all the way home.

CHAPTER 11

EVERYTHING YOU WANTED TO KNOW ABOUT OUTFITTERS

Every year, a few thousand elk hunters make the startling discovery that outfitted hunts aren't necessarily easy. Some turn out that way, but most don't. One perception among the unknowing is that all you do is ride your horse through the woods, locate an elk, get off the horse, shoot the elk, and let the outfitter and guides worry about dressing it and packing it down to your vehicle or to a meat processor.

This all sounds good, and I wish it was the case, but it ain't, folks. You might come home from that hunt with more aching bones and muscles than from hunts you did on your own. Of course, many outfitted hunts indeed turn out to be easy, but many do not.

Should you hire an outfitter? The decision to pay for his services depends on a number of factors. There are advantages and disadvantages, with good arguments on each side.

Perhaps the most important advantage is less competition from other hunters. This is possible *only* because the outfitter provides *access*, which can be either physical or legal. Horses and mules are necessary to transport people and gear into remote regions. Without saddle and pack animals, the only choice is to hike and carry essential items on your back. That gets old in a hurry, particularly if you're not in excellent physical condition and aren't

capable of walking along trails in the western mountains—most of which seem to be leading uphill.

The legal aspect pertains to private ground that the outfitter owns or leases. Without him, those lands are unavailable to you. Therefore, access translates directly to competition. As with all forms of hunting, you'll have a far better hunt the farther you get from people. That's not true in fishing—you can have a whale of a good time in a crowd if the fish are biting. Therein lies the difference between the two activities.

The trek to remote mountainous regions isn't made because outfitters like to lead folks 15 or 20 miles into the outback. It's a fact of life that some of the best elk hunting is in places difficult to reach; your odds are often better in backcountry areas.

It's possible to rent horses and make a trip on your own, but be advised that you'd better know how to pack. Unless you have the savvy to tie the correct knots and load a horse or mule properly, forget a do-it-yourself trip where pack animals are involved. Packing is a science; if you haven't quite mastered it, you'll cuss the day you planned the trip.

Another reason to hire an outfitter is to take advantage of his knowledge. He should know practically every trail in his territory, and he should know which high country regions produce game. He should put you onto ridges and basins that produce the best big game hunting, leaving the guesswork out. That's not to say, of course, that your success is guaranteed. Too many factors can influence a hunting trip. About all an outfitter can do is try his best to make your experience a productive one. Unfortunately, some outfitters fail miserably in their operations. Many are phonies, and would do a better service to humanity flipping burgers in a fast food joint.

You'll definitely appreciate an outfitter when it's time to transport your animal out of the backcountry. His services almost always include field-dressing, transporting the meat to camp, and hauling it out to your vehicle or to a meat processor where you can make arrangements to have it delivered to your home.

A mature bull elk will weigh 650 pounds to a half-ton on the hoof. If you quarter a bull, which is a standard procedure, you'll be hefting quarters that tip the scales at 90 pounds or more. And the chore of reducing an elk to quarters is often a grueling task in itself. If you do it on your own, be aware that you'll have earned

the meat the hard way, and you may never again make an attempt on an elk's life unless a road is handy or downhill, or both. You'll swear that the knives and saws intended for cutting up an elk were invented by sadists who enjoy human suffering, and you'll be convinced that an elk's bones are made of steel. The bottom line is it just ain't fun, or even possible, for some folks to move 400 or more pounds of meat through the mountain landscape, most of which will be designed to make the task as nasty as can be.

An outfitter will pack you and your gear into a remote area where elk are abundant.

A final advantage in teaming up with an outfitter is having a bit of comfort around hunting camp. A cook will prepare and serve your meals, a wrangler or guide will tend to your horse, and you'll have a place to sleep. Tents, normally equipped with cots and woodstoves, will allow you to maintain some degree of protection from the elements, which can suddenly make life miserable. Autumn weather is fickle in the West. You can count on anything. In some areas, cabins may be used, or a ranch house, or even a motel. Every outfitter has different accommodations.

Once you get your elk, your outfitter will pack your elk down to the trailhead or to a meat processor in town.

Here's a tip if you'll be sleeping in a tent. Rest assured the inside temperature of the tent will match that of the outside once the fire in the wood stove goes out after you crawl in the sleeping bag. The fire *will* go out, by the way. Most stoves are good for about three to four hours. Some hunters are unaware of this little fact, and bring summer sleeping bags. That's a colossal mistake, because you'll freeze half to death and be miserable in the morning if the night air is cold, which it's apt to be in elk country. An option is to keep the fire going all night, which is another big pain. Avoid all this hassle by bringing along a warm sleeping bag in the first place, and be sure to sleep on some sort of pad, especially if you're on a cot. Your weight compresses the bottom of the bag, eliminating the loft, and the best arctic bag you can buy will be worthless if you're on a cot.

The obvious disadvantage to hiring an outfitter is the cost, but don't be surprised if the expense of a do-it-yourself trip closely matches that of a guided outing. By the time you buy the necessary gear, food, and figure transportation, your savings might be lower than anticipated. Currently, an outfitted hunt will cost $500

to $800 or more a day, depending on the type and length of the hunt, and other factors. The fee usually covers pickup and return to a nearby airport, food, lodging, horses, and transportation of meat. You'll be expected to purchase your own hunting license and bring your own sleeping bag, firearm, ammo, and personal items.

DROP CAMPS

If you want an economical outfitted hunt, consider a drop-camp, but be aware of the pitfalls. At first, a drop camp sounds like a good deal. You and your pals will be transported on horseback by an outfitter to a backcountry camp, and you'll be dropped off for a week. Camp consists of a big wall tent, woodstove, cooking stove, lantern, cots and other accessories. You'll be on your own to hunt; the outfitter will return to pick you and your elk or deer up at the end of the hunt. More good news—all this for only $750 or so.

Too good to be true? That depends entirely on the integrity of the outfitter. You may be in for a dream or nightmare hunt.

Horses and mules are the key to packing gear to remote camps.

If my mail is any indication of reader's complaints, I'd have to put the drop camp at the top of the list. Rip-offs are common, and plenty of hunters are bilked by shameless outfitters. Most hunters are more upset with the time lost than the money. What they perceived to be a great hunt ended up as a squandered experience.

Here's a true horror story. Four hunters arrive at the designated meeting spot and the outfitter is nowhere around. After two hours, a guide finally shows up and admits he was just hired and had never been to the drop camp area. The agreement included food to be provided, but there was none. The hunters bought groceries, and after a six-hour late start, they got lost in the dark, and finally rode in to camp at midnight. The tent was ripped apart by the wind, there was no firewood, and a snowstorm had just blown in. The hunters never saw an elk though they tried hard, and the hunt was a total bust.

Many outfitters don't offer drop camps because there's little profit margin, and the outlay of time and equipment to set up camps and transport hunters in and out can't be justified. Profits are highest with fully guided hunters who will pay anywhere from $2,500 to $4,000 or more, depending on the outfitter. Most drop camp hunts average $750 to $1,000.

Unfortunately, some outfitters provide drop camps in marginal areas where game is scarce or nonexistent. Therein lies the basis for complaints. Hunters see little or no game, realizing they've been had.

It's easy to understand why many outfitters keep drop camp hunters out of their prime hunting grounds. Those choice areas are reserved for the high paying hunters who use guide services. Obviously, the outfitter wants no competition from other hunters in those fertile hunting spots, and makes sure he sets the drop camp hunters far enough away so they won't interfere. An outfitter has enough of a problem competing with the general public (unless he's hunting private land), and isn't about to generate more. Some outfitters, on the other hand, can effectively keep a decent buffer between both camps and offer good hunting potential all the way around.

And what about hunters who book a drop camp to learn the land for future hunts on their own? Sort of like the angler who hires a guide for a day to learn the water; then fishes every day afterward in those hotspots by himself. Makes good sense, if you're willing to fork out the initial fee.

Most outfitters are aware that some hardy hunters might return with their own equipment. I've heard of cases where hunters actually camped within a few yards of the drop camp they'd booked previously. That's intense competition. It's understandable, then, that some decent outfitters want nothing to do with drop camps.

Some outfitters have several dozen horses. Pack animals are a vital aspect of the backcountry elk camp.

Then you have the unethical outfitter who sees nothing wrong in placing drop camps everywhere he can, even where elk are nonexistent, and then advertising them to be the hottest spots in the state. Nonresident hunters unfamiliar with the area have no clue they're booking a hunt in a barren place. They're happy to have a place to hunt in a strange area far from home, and what the hell, the price is right.

I'm not implying that all drop camps are run by shady characters. I've been on plenty of drop camp hunts, most good, a few not so good.

Humans being what they are, you can't please all the people all the time. I know of a drop camp hunter who demanded he be refunded his money because three feet of snow dumped on his camp and so he did not want to hunt. Snow was not part of the

package, he claimed. Another hunter whined because he shot an elk on the first day and had nothing to do the rest of the hunt. Most hunters wish they could have such a problem.

How do you tell if you're booking a drop camp with a reputable outfitter? Common sense suggests you contact past references, but this is seldom effective because the outfitter only lists happy campers. If he booked 80 hunters in a year and 78 were convinced the outfitter was a jerk, you can bet he'll give you the names of the two satisfied hunters. (They were probably satisfied because they blundered into a rare elk and managed to score).

When contacting references, call rather than write. Most people don't write their own mothers, and you'll get far more information on the phone. Ask your source for the names and phone numbers of other hunters in camp, because people tend to trade business cards. You'll get a better cross-section of the hunting party.

A call to the game department may not be productive, because most agencies are unwilling to divulge negative information on an outfitter for legal reasons. Some agencies are not allowed to do so, period. What you *can* learn, however, is if the outfitter is properly licensed. If not, do yourself a big favor and forget this guy immediately. You might be headed for trouble with the law yourself, as well as having a lousy hunt.

A fair question to ask the outfitter is the location of the *general* drop camp area. Note the word *general*. Imagine what would happen if you asked him to pinpoint the area. It won't happen. Most outfitters didn't fall off the turnip truck. If you can indeed learn the general area, check with the game department and inquire as to the hunting potential of the location.

It would be helpful to learn the hunter success rate of past hunters in the drop camp you're considering, but it's often misleading information, reflecting the skills of the hunters rather than the potential of the area. This is also true for a regular outfitted hunt. For example, say four hunters killed one elk. The success rate is 25 percent. What that doesn't tell you is that two of the hunters missed their shots, and one was so out of shape he never traveled more than 300 yards from camp. For this reason, outfitters are reluctant to give success rate figures. A more fair question would be to ask how many shooting *opportunities* hunters had experienced.

An appropriate question is to ask the quality of the game in the area the outfitter hunts. If you're hoping for a bull elk that scores 300 Boone and Crockett points, you should know if the area produces animals of that stature. Any outfitter with integrity will tell you. If he doesn't, or dances around the question, write him off your list. Believe me, there are many, many places in the west where elk that score 300 or better do not exist. As pointed elsewhere in this book (many times), it takes years for a bull to grow massive antlers. Some places have enough pressure that the big boys are never produced.

These hunters follow a guide, who will take them to good spots. Sometimes a daily ride several miles from camp is required.

Some drop-camp outfitters offer a variety of services, such as those who have a bare-bones package where you bring your own food. He provides a sleeping/cooking tent, a supply of firewood, utensils, and cooking and heating stoves. You ride horseback to camp, and are left to hunt on foot. Another package includes a camp cook/grunt who keeps camp tidy and food on the table. Yet another comes with a wrangler or guide who stays with you, providing horses.

The majority of drop camps are the inexpensive variety. If you book one of these, do yourself a big favor and count on Murphy's Law being omnipresent. Take nothing for granted and be prepared.

Simple examples: you arrive at camp and the axe handle is busted, or the lantern mantles are deteriorated, or there's not enough propane for the cookstove. These aren't big worries under normal situations, but they become monumental when you have no replacements and you're stuck in the boonies for a week with no light, heat, or cooking fuel. Be smart. Bring your own gear.

In addition to personal gear, my list includes a lightweight plastic tarp that you can throw on the roof of a leaky tent (always assume your tent will leak); a two burner campstove and extra fuel; a lantern and extra fuel; a foam sleeping pad, a sharp axe, and a complete first aid kit.

Because you'll probably be dragging into camp late every day and will be in no mood to cook, bring pre-cooked, frozen meals that you've prepared at home. Good meals that defrost easily are chili, stews, casseroles, baked chicken, and meat loaf. For a treat, bring along some frozen, uncooked steaks.

Be sure you know the weight limitations, since horseback travel may require you to trim your meals. Bring the food in coolers and ask the outfitter to pack them in. Otherwise, he'll put the food in panniers (saddle-pack containers), and after he departs you'll have no way to protect food from heat and rodents while in camp.

Insist on maps of the area around camp. If the outfitter doesn't provide them, be sure to buy them at a local sporting goods store before you head in to camp. Since you're on your own, you'll naturally want updated maps.

Find out exactly how your meat will be handled. Some outfitters request that you transport it to camp, and some will pick it up at the site of the kill. If you need to move several hundred pounds of elk meat, or a heavy deer a mile or two in the mountains, you'll need adequate gear. I use a portable one-wheeled carrier that's easily dismantled and packed on a horse. It's saved the day a dozen times when I was faced with transporting a moose, elk, or deer. The other option is carrying it out on your back if you have no horses. Trust me, it's far easier to roll a load on wheels than to lug it on your back.

Spend some time doing your homework before booking a drop camp. That "deal" you thought was so great might come back to haunt you.

Many hunters prefer to hire outfitters to take them to drop camps. Author's pal, Garry Day, adjusts the lantern in this camp tent.

FINDING AN OUTFITTER

How do you select an ethical outfitter for either a drop camp or regular hunt? One way is to check the listings in the "where-to-go" sections of outdoor magazines, write to a number of outfitters, and request a list of references. Call the references rather than write; you'll learn much more on the phone. Another option is to meet with outfitters at the major sport shows. A third is to work with a reliable booking agent. There's no charge for this service, and a good agent will be able to direct you to the outfitter best-equipped to meet your needs and expectations. Finally, you can buy a hunt at auctions hosted by the Rocky Mountain Elk Foundation, often at bargain prices. These auctions are held at the hundreds of chapter fund-raisers around the country, as well as at the national convention. Safari Club International and The Foundation for North American Wild Sheep also have auctions at their national and regional conventions.

An important disadvantage to hunting with an outfitter, though one that can be easily resolved, is the necessity to keep up the pace set by your guide. Most western guides are young, tough cowboys

who can walk and climb all day and make the effort seem like child's play. Unless you communicate to him the fact that you're not in the same league as he is you'll have a rough time, and your hunt may well turn into an ordeal. Guides don't intentionally try to kill off their hunters—there's just plenty of ground to cover, and time is often of the essence when trying to reach prime game country. This is why I alluded to the fact that outfitted hunts are not necessarily easy. In some cases you can do a lot of hunting on a horse, but invariably you'll tie the horse to a tree and hunt on foot for a good part of the day. You may find yourself thinking: "I'm paying good money for *this*?"

It may not look like much, but this tent with its wood stove will keep the hunters snug and cozy. Be aware that when the fire dies out in the night, a warm sleeping bag is a good idea!

Hunting on your own allows you to set your own speed and select your own hours. You can sleep as long as you want, and hunt according to your personal requirements. You can, of course, do the same on an outfitted trip, but you'll no doubt want to get the most out of the experience, which means sleeping little, hunting a lot, and feeling sorry for yourself when your out-of-shape body protests.

To some people, completing a project without professional assistance is important. These are folks who repair and maintain their own automobiles, or fix their plumbing leaks and electrical problems. Self-sufficient indoors as well as outdoors, they are willing to accept the hardships of doing it on their own, and realize a great deal of personal satisfaction by doing so. To them, hiring an outfitter is the easy way out.

Whether you hire an outfitter depends on your personal requirements. You must determine your capability to make a backcountry trip, and decide whether you can afford the cost of a hunt. But, and I repeat, do not consider this an easy hunt if you're hunting horseback in the mountains. Of course, a hunt on a private ranch from a four wheel drive pickup truck is another matter, but there's still no guarantee. Your dream bull might be staring at you halfway up a mountain, and the only way up is to hike. There goes your easy hunt.

This hunter has set up a small camp in an area he will bowhunt. Note the grouse hanging over the tent that will help offset the cost of food.

Chapter 12

You Can Hunt Elk for $500

If you think you can't afford to hunt elk because it's too expensive, take a closer look. With careful planning and a willingness to be thrifty, you can indeed make a hunt that won't ravage your bank account.

First off, you should choose your companions carefully. Nothing can ruin a trip quicker than a member of the group who doesn't fit in with the others. Each hunter should have the same expectations, and be willing to abide by a frugal budget as well as any minor discomforts caused by your economy plan.

Let's assume you live 2,000 miles from Colorado, where you intend to hunt. I'm selecting Colorado as an example because it's the only major elk state where nonresidents can buy an elk tag across the counter. Other states require a lottery draw or first-come first-served system. Colorado's nonresident elk tag is also among the cheapest in the west; $250.25 as this book is written. (It will reportedly be increased to come into parity with other states in a couple of years. The average general fee for other states is between $450 and $500.) Colorado also has 11 national forests with more than 14 million acres of public land, more than any other state in elk country. If you intend to hunt another state, you may have to pay more for an elk tag.

Considering ideal space limitations, three hunters are optimum. This number works best when driving to and from your hunt, and when camping. Let's say you're going hunting with George and Jack.

Plan your hunt well. This hunter is camped in a public campground and is studying maps to determine a hunting strategy.

Once you've determined who your companions will be, you need to decide whose vehicle you'll use. In my opinion, a 4wd is a must in elk country, and it should be equipped with a sturdy jack, four chains, jumper cables, tow chain, and other routine gear. We'll assume that one of you has such a rig and is willing to put several thousand miles on it.

To meet your budget, you'll need to camp and hunt on public land. A small camp cost may be incurred if you camp in a U.S. Forest Service designated campground, but many are available for free during hunting season. In most national forests you can merely camp at no charge in a place that strikes your fancy. Be sure you know the rules, and buy a map of the forest you're hunting (around $4).

Choose a camp shelter you already own, but be aware that in elk country you can always expect extremely cold weather. Most hunters own some sort of camp rig, whether it's a tent, camp trailer, pickup cab-over camper, van, motorhome, etc. In the case of the latter, consider towing a hunting vehicle, but remember that the cost of fuel for a motorhome can be considerably higher than that for a pickup or sport utility vehicle.

Sit down with your buddies at a planning session before your trip and determine who can provide essential camping gear, such as cookstoves, lanterns, axes, utensils, first aid kit, and other necessary items. Most hunters already own such equipment. To trans-

port an elk out of the woods, you'll also need sturdy backpacks, a sharp saw and knife, rope, meat sacks, etc. You may need to spend a few dollars to buy items such as extra lantern mantles, propane, lantern fuel, etc. You'll also need items such as toilet paper, paper towels, paper plates, plastic utensils, and dishwashing soap. You can save money by using real plates and silverware, but you'll obviously need to wash them. Let's say you'll spend $75 for paper goods and camp supplies, at a shared cost of $25 each.

When considering food, we're going to assume that it's not an extra expense. Look at it this way: wherever you are, you must eat, whether you're hunting, at home, or on the job. If you'll purchase your food when it's on sale before the hunt and store or freeze it, you'll save plenty of money. For example, I buy chicken leg quarters on sale at $.49 per pound, cook and freeze them. I also cook chili, stew, lasagna, and other foods that are easily frozen, using venison from the freezer to cut down on the expense of buying meat. In fact, I use wild game exclusively. Granted, it's not free when you consider the cost of hunting, but it's not added to your elk hunting budget. I freeze those meals until I'm ready to hunt, and keep the frozen food in coolers and thaw it as required. All you need to do is heat it when you come in from hunting. Before your planning session, snoop around your pantry and grab some canned or packaged foods that you can pool together. You'll likely find some dusty cans of fruit, soup and vegetables that need to be eaten soon. Everything will taste better in elk camp after long, grueling days.

A compact camp like this will offer you plenty of comfort and still be inexpensive.

On your trip to elk country, take turns driving. One person should stay awake with the driver to keep him company. Lodging should not be part of your trip cost. If everyone is sleepy, pull over in a highway rest area for several hours. If you *really* want a bed to stretch out in and a shower, rent an inexpensive motel room. You should be able to rent a room with two beds and bring in a rollaway bed for under $50. You'll likely be driving on interstate highways most of the way, and the current legal speed limit of 75 mph on most roads will allow you to zing right along.

Getting your elk cut up and moved out of the woods can be a major chore but if you plan well and have adequate tools, you can get the job done.

Meals on the road should be considered with your budget in mind. For breakfast I have coffee, juice, and a pastry. I bring along a cooler with assorted cold cuts, lettuce, ketchup, mustard, etc. to make sandwiches for lunch, and for dinner I look for a place with a big salad bar that goes with the meal. Instead of a T-bone, I eat a chicken-fried steak, a pop, or coffee for a total cost of around $8 to $9.

Gasoline for your rig will be a major expense. Let's say you drive 2,000 miles each way and another 500 miles while hunting. That's 4,500 miles. Figuring your vehicle gets 12 miles per gallon, you'll buy 375 gallons of gasoline at an average of $1.30 per gallon, for a total of about $488. Split three ways, that's around $163 each. Add another $10 each for motor oil, coolant, and windshield wiper fluid.

Of course, the person who owns the vehicle will accrue "wear and tear" expenses. Tires and parts wear down, and the extra mileage decreases the vehicle's value. Let's simplify matters and work it this way. Say George uses his vehicle for the elk hunt. For the rest of the year on other hunting and/or fishing trips, you and Jack will use your vehicles. It doesn't take a lot of trips for avid outdoorsmen to drive plenty of miles, even fairly close to home. The next time you make a long distance trip, another person should do the driving.

Before you leave on the trip, everyone should put $100 in a kitty. A designated banker holds the money. All trip costs, except for personal items such as medicine, toilet items, and gifts, should come from the bank. When the bank is getting low, everyone tosses in another equal amount. In this way, you don't need to keep complicated records on who paid for gasoline last, or meals, and how much.

Many hunters are self-sufficient. You can do all your cooking at camp and save money.

Assuming the nights are cool, which is almost a guarantee in elk country, you shouldn't have problems chilling your elk meat. Normally, you shouldn't need to rent space in a walk-in cooler. Wrap the chilled meat tightly in old, clean quilts or sleeping bags as you travel home. It should stay cold for two days or more. If you stop to sleep during the trip, loosen the covering and allow the cool night air to circulate, but don't expose it entirely. Stray roadside cats will enjoy sharing it with you.

If you'll follow these suggestions, here's what your approximate cost per person will amount to: Elk tag: $250; camp supplies: $25; and gasoline and vehicle costs: $173, for a total of $448. Remember, a bare-bones hunt might require some extra sacrifice, but this plan works. Besides doing it myself, I know several hunters who save plenty of money each year. Indeed, an elk hunt could be easily within your reach.

Learn how to cape your elk so you can do it yourself. A number of videos show the step by step process.

CHAPTER 13

THE DO-IT-YOURSELF HUNT

Most elk hunters who don't live in elk country will not hire an outfitter. They'll hunt on their own, typically on public land. Consequently, there's always those nagging questions that must be answered. Where do you hunt, and how do you find information? Outlined here are some of the basics that should help you get started.

First you must choose a state, then narrow your search to an area within it. If you're at square one and have no idea which state to hunt, read big game editions of outdoor magazines. Published in late summer each year, they report on hunting prospects in each state, along with the best places to go, regulations, seasons, fees, and application procedures.

Don't be misled by the data on population or total harvest. The important criterion is the hunter success rate, which is always figured on a percentage basis. For example, if a state had a general success rate of 23 percent for elk, that means 23 out of 100 hunters took an elk, and those figures usually include antlerless elk in the totals.

This figure doesn't always tell the truth, because states often lump all hunts together. Nor does it indicate the success rate for specific areas, or for restricted hunts, or "quality" hunts. You need to dig for that information. Take Colorado, for example. This state

91

Pay attention to the vehicle you'll be taking. A 4wd pickup is standard, but it can get you stuck, too!

has the highest elk population in the West, but offers only an average hunter success rate. However, there are units in the state that offer outstanding hunting opportunities, with hunter success rates at 50 percent and higher. Those units require a lottery draw; there is plenty of competition for tags. If you can draw a tag in one of those units, you can enjoy hunting as good as any in the West. I've mentioned those lottery draw hunts a great deal in this book, because they are the key to an easy elk.

In some states hunter success figures are public information, but in others you must ask. That's where your research should start.

USE THE PHONE

Don't write for all your information. You'll get many more details over the phone. Initial sources of information are state wildlife agencies. Start by calling the headquarters office (telephone numbers listed state-by-state are listed in the Appendix) to find out the telephone number of the regional office in the area you've selected. (States are divided into regions, with a central office in each.) Ask to talk to a big game biologist, game warden, environmental specialist, or whoever is available. Foresters and wildlife biologists with federal land management agencies, particularly the U.S. Forest Service and Bureau of Land Management,

can be very helpful as well.

Be as inquisitive as you can, and don't be timid. If you're stymied by an officious-sounding receptionist who won't allow you to speak to an employee, ask if hunting success figures are public information. If so, tell him or her what you're interested in, and request the best means of obtaining the information you want.

Some individuals who work for government agencies aren't fond of answering hunter's questions, but most will open up to you if you're polite and not overly aggressive. I worked as a forester and wildlife biologist for state and federal agencies for sixteen years, and welcomed the opportunity to chat with hunters who requested information. It was a refreshing break from a routine that often involved boring desk projects, and I enjoyed talking with hunters who were astute enough to seek information for a do-it-yourself hunt.

Always plan on the necessity of getting your meat out. Can you carry each of these 95 pound quarters out of the woods?

ASK THE RIGHT QUESTIONS

Here are some specific questions to ask when researching hunting areas.

"What is the hunter success rate?" Areas with a rate of 25 percent or less should be looked upon with skepticism. One out of four isn't good; try for units that have 40 percent or better. If you're

hunting a western state, find out if the percentages are skewed by outfitters in the area. Many outfitters have very high success hunts, while hunters on their own have very low success hunts. The reason is the outfitter's ability to pack into remote regions, his knowledge of game country, and his private land hunts.

The fact that you're a nonresident doesn't necessarily mean you'll have poor success, however. It's a fact that nonresident hunters have far higher success rates than residents when the two are compared on non-outfitted hunts. The reason is nonresidents simply try harder, hunt longer, and invest more money in a hunt. Residents often hunt on weekends or make one-day forays.

Author carries the rack and some of the boned elk meat out to a road. The weight of this load is about 80 pounds.

"What kind of access do the units have?" The answer to this question will determine your ability to travel in the unit, and will provide insight to competition from other hunters. Areas riddled by roads will no doubt have plenty of hunter pressure. This information will also help you determine the kind of vehicle you'll need. Some hunting units may be accessible only by way of 4wd vehicles.

"What are the opportunities for taking a trophy-class animal?" If a big rack interests you, this is the first question you should ask. Wildlife officers can often give accurate statistics, especially if

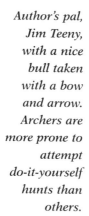
Author's pal, Jim Teeny, with a nice bull taken with a bow and arrow. Archers are more prone to attempt do-it-yourself hunts than others.

game-check stations have been active in the areas for a number of years. Many states keep records of trophy-class animals and the units where they're taken. Some states have their own version of trophy-class rankings based on Boone and Crockett measurement procedures.

So far these questions are general. If the wildlife officer you're speaking with is cordial and doesn't mind volunteering information, try these specific questions:

"Where would *you* hunt for a good chance at a legal animal?"

"Where would *you* hunt for a good chance at a trophy-class animal?"

In both cases, make it clear that you aren't interested in learning the wildlife officer's personal hotspots. He or she isn't going to tell you anyway. The two key words in the questions are "good chance". They give your contact some leeway, and you won't sound pushy. You'd be treading on hallowed ground if you asked, "Where do *you* Hunt?"

"How much public land is available?" You'll need to know how much land you can actually hunt on. If you're planning to hunt a national forest, you'll have plenty of acreage to roam. But you're not assured of a place to hunt just because there are blocks of

national forest or Bureau of Land Management lands interspersed with private lands. In many cases, early homesteaders settled in the fertile valley bottoms and ignored the peripheral mountains. Today, those private lands will likely be fenced and posted, and though the best hunting may be on public land in the surrounding mountains, access may be effectively blocked because of locked private gates in the valleys. This is a major problem in much of the West.

"Do any private landowners allow access, either free or for a trespass fee?" Much of the best hunting is on private land for obvious reasons. Hunting is restricted, and game is less disturbed than on public land. These days it's tough to find private landowners who will allow you to hunt for free, particularly if you're a nonresident.

Expensive leases are the rule instead of the exception in many states, and leasing has caught on big in the West. In Colorado, for example, you'd be hard pressed to find a rancher who will allow you to hunt at no charge; the best areas are leased long in advance of hunting season by groups of hunters or outfitters. Nonetheless, there are ranchers who will let you on for free or a modest trespass fee. You'll have to look hard to find them.

When hunting on your own, hunt smart and pay attention to the country around you. It's up to you to spot and stalk elk since you can't count on any help.

You're more apt to find free or inexpensive hunting on private lands where big game animals damage crops, but don't count on it. Some states offer landowners different incentives to allow

THE DO-IT-YOURSELF HUNT   97

Zumbo and one of his best hunting pals, Tony Knight, president of Modern Muzzle Loading, Inc. -- makers of Knight Firearms. Hunt only with compatible buddies.

access. In Wyoming, for example, landowners are given a coupon, which is attached to the license, when you kill an animal on their property. He or she turns the coupon in to a game warden and is paid $8 for each animal harvested. The system has its advantages: The rancher is happy because he is reimbursed for some of the crop damage caused by big game animals, and he in turn is apt to allow hunting on his property. The hunter is happy because of increased hunting opportunities.

The best way to find out about hunting private land is the old-fashioned way. Walk up to the door and knock. If the landowner says no, ask if there are other farmers or ranchers in the area that might allow hunting. Obviously this is one method of locating new hunting areas that you can't do by phone or by mail, unless you have some advance information. It's always best to ask permission in person if you're dealing with strangers. Of course, your telephone research will enable you to get as much information as possible before you make your visit.

APPLY EARLY

Once you've settled on an area, be sure to apply early for a license if there's a deadline or quota. In most states, you can buy a big game license prior to or during the season, but in the West

the best states require a lottery draw or operate on a first-come-first-serve system for nonresidents. In Wyoming, for example, nonresident elk applications must be in by January 31. In Idaho and Montana, there is a quota on nonresident elk tags; they're sold on a first-come basis. Lately Montana has had more applicants than tags, so a lottery is used.

You'll receive no sympathy from a state agency if your application is late. It will be firmly rejected, so pay attention to application instructions.

SCOUT SMART

If you've done your homework right, and if you've drawn a permit (if a lottery was required), your next job is to find out all you can about the country you intend to hunt.

Again, the phone will be your best research tool. Be sure to have a pencil and pad handy to record the information you obtain. The purpose of your initial telephone conversations was to locate general hunting areas. Now you need to focus in on ridges, valleys, drainages, and precise spots within the hunting unit. Use the same sources that you used before to ferret out as much information as possible.

A basic requirement is to get the most detailed, up-to-date maps you can find. The U.S. Forest Service has maps for each of their national forests across the country, and the Bureau of Land Management has state and district maps. Write to each agency and ask for the maps they have available. Some maps are free, others cost $4 or less. Aside from public land maps that show major drainages, land boundaries, and roads, you should order topographic maps published by the U.S. Geological Survey. Their maps show details the others don't, including contours, tiny drainages, pack and old jeep trails, marshes, and other features that could help you plan your hunt. For maps east of the Mississippi, write the U.S. Geological Survey, 536 National Center, Reston, VA 22092; for maps west of the Mississippi, write the U.S. Geological Survey, Box 25046, Federal Center, Denver, CO 80225.

Study the maps, and with the information you've obtained by talking to agency employees, circle the areas they mentioned. Jot down the names of roads in the map margin, and any other references. When you're done, you should have a map with several options drawn on it, and some sort of strategy in mind.

Choose your companions carefully when you plan a hunt. Author poses here with two of his favorite hunting pals, Garry and Bert Day.

If possible, do scout the area before hunting season. This is common advice, but few hunters follow it. Remember, up to now you have information from phone conversations and a few maps. The next and final step before hunting is to physically look over the land and make some basic decisions about where you'll hunt.

Before you scout, make it a point to stop at the wildlife or forest agency office to get as much updated information as possible. Ask about the condition of the roads, places to camp, and once again ask about areas to hunt in. When you drive to the unit, talk to ranchers, farmers, forest workers, loggers, surveyors, sheepherders, and anyone else who might be able to give you first-hand information.

If you have time, corroborate the information you've received with locals. Go to a sporting goods store and chat with clerks. Get a haircut and talk to the barber. Have a beer or a soft drink in a local tavern and talk with the patrons and bartender. This might seem to be an exercise in futility; as an outsider you may feel like the locals are putting you on. That's the case now and then, but generally folks are sincere and try to help. A last-minute inquiry might prove to be the best move you made.

You can't do too much planning for a hunt. The more the better, and the result of your work could very well be a handsome animal that you'll always cherish. And your hunt will be a whole heck of a lot easier if you plan well.

Author with a nice bull he took on the Vermejo Ranch, which is one of the most famous in the west.

CHAPTER 14

THE TRUTH ABOUT RANCH HUNTING

Just what is an elk ranch? Let's not confuse this operation with a game farm, surrounded by a high fence, which is also sometimes called an elk ranch (those high fenced operations are covered in another chapter). What we're referring to here is a private property that is unfenced and usually large enough to hold elk.

The West has thousands of such ranches, some of which are well known, and some of which are obscure. Examples of the more famous ones include the Vermejo in New Mexico, owned by Ted Turner, the Flying D in Montana, also owned by Turner, the Taylor Ranch in Colorado, the Deseret in Utah, and many more. Most of these ranches offer limited hunting, and you can bet the prices are high, often in the five digit range.

But for every large, well-known ranch, there are hundreds of others. Most, unfortunately, no longer offer free hunting if they allow hunting at all. These properties are typically leased to outfitters or groups of hunters.

A look at the western landscape reveals an interesting dilemma for hunters. Back in the days when we settled the West, homesteaders logically chose fertile lands in valley bottoms where soil was better for grazing and growing crops, and water was available. They left the higher elevations, which were basically incorporated into the federal system, primarily the U.S. Forest Service and the Bureau of Land Management.

Looking at those lands today is confusing, because of the patchwork of intermingled private and public lands. In every state, small parcels of private land effectively block access to larger tracts of public land. No matter how hard you try to gain legal access, you'll probably fail because the system does not require landowners to open avenues across their property to those federal acres.

There are some great ranches and some that are mediocre. George Taulman of United States Outfitters, pictured here, runs some of the best ranch hunts in New Mexico.

So we have an unfortunate situation where hunters are locked out simply because someone owns a few acres along a road and refuses public access. Making the matter worse is the law in some states that requires the public to know where they are at all times because landowners don't have to post their property. What this means is that you'd better have a good map and know how to read it, because you'll be in serious trouble if you trespass, even though you've made an honest mistake.

When I first moved west in 1960, I could knock on a rancher's door and invariably get permission to hunt, as well as a cup of coffee and a piece of homemade pie. Unfortunately, those days are gone forever, because hunters began to realize that they could have their little bit of heaven on earth by offering the rancher money and having his ranch exclusively theirs to hunt. Outfitters

quickly caught on, and lined up to compete for the rights to hunt the best ranches. By 1980, most ranches in prime elk and deer country were leased; today virtually all of it is leased in states like Colorado, New Mexico, Utah, and others.

To hunt those ranches, you'll have to join up with a group of hunters who lease them, or book with the outfitter who has the hunting rights on it. Another option is for your son or daughter to marry into the rancher's family, and hope you'll get permission to hunt!

Just how good will the hunting be? You can expect the extremes, from awful to fantastic, depending, of course, on the size of the ranch, access to the elk on it, and the number and quality of elk.

Here are some problems to look out for. Some ranches are in low elevations, where elk may be nonexistent until serious snow forces them to lower country. You can hunt your heart out and never see a living, breathing, elk. Some ranches are overshot because greedy outfitters and landowners allow too many hunters to take too many elk. That being the case, the elk you'll find will be essentially made up of spikes, raghorns (four and five-point bulls), and maybe a spindly six-pointer.

Jim Zumbo with a good southwest bull taken on a big ranch. Note the fairly gentle terrain here, making this hunt a bit easier than most.

Some ranches may offer several seasons, as in Colorado and New Mexico. The hunts during the first seasons may be okay, but elk wise up quickly and may be tough to find later. I know many hunters who have hunted some of the big ranches and had bad experiences because most of the elk were either shot or educated. As I mentioned, maybe the late hunt is the *only* time you'll see an elk on the property.

Bottom line here is this: just because you're hunting private property, don't set your sights too high. That bull you thought would be easy may just be a fleeting fantasy.

Be on the lookout for phony outfitters. Get solid references from years past. Too many outfitters will beat hell out of a ranch with no regard to the future, then move on to another one once their dirty work is done. That's not to say all outfitters are selfish. Many understand how to maintain quality hunting, and are willing to book fewer hunters, even though it won't rapidly fatten their bank accounts by doing so.

And remember that private land often offers better hunting simply because there is less competition. Any time you reduce hunting pressure, you have more available animals, as well as older animals, since more will survive hunting season. Older means bigger antlers, if indeed you're looking for a good bull.

Chapter 15

The Basics of Calling

Who doesn't correlate bugling with elk? This is a thrilling sound, one of the most exciting vocalizations in all the outdoors. But, it must be remembered that most elk hunters will hear very little or no bugling, simply because it occurs primarily during the breeding season.

I've come to the conclusion that bugling reaches its peak right around September 22nd, which happens to be the first day of fall, (and my wife's birthday), plus or minus a week. Breeding activity may start as early as late August, and extend well into October. You can hear bugling any time during that period.

Big problem—many rifle hunts start in mid to late October, when vocalization is over. Bowhunters have the best of it; with all states offering elk bow seasons during the rut.

There are some options to rifle hunters who want to hunt the bugle season, such as limited entry hunts with special early hunts, and in many wilderness areas, where September rifle hunts are common.

But just because you're out there during prime time, that doesn't mean the elk will come running (as depicted on the cover of this book). Many factors come into play—elk can be elusive and frustrating to hunt during the breeding season. Consider the following experience I had.

The Selway wilderness is quiet, except for the muted sounds of a remote creek somewhere off in the distance. It is September 25, prime time for elk to be calling, but we hear absolutely nothing. It's one of those times when elk are silent. As I like to say, they're having a serious case of lockjaw.

We're doing everything you're supposed to do on a backwoods elk hunt. My guide and I are in the saddles at least an hour before the first glow of light in the eastern sky. Riding through total blackness, under huge stands of fir and spruce, we hear nothing in the forest as each day is born, other than the barking of irritated red squirrels and hungry ravens squawking above the timbered canopy.

This part of Idaho is no place for the hunter who likes seeing elk in lovely parks and meadows, because there are none. The vast Selway is the most challenging chunk of elk country I've ever been in. Every time I go there I swear I'll never go back, but I know down deep I don't really mean it. There's something about this busted up, steep, blowdown jungle that keeps me returning for more. A certain mystique, if you will, that calls to your brain, ignoring all the other hunts in that miserable place that caused you pain and suffering.

So here we are, tying our horses to trees on a small ridge, and soon descending into the bowels of a valley so heavily timbered that you would take bets that no elk could possibly get around. Yet you see piles of droppings here and there, and the occasional freshly rubbed tree spurs you on.

My guide is an affable chap, born and raised in elk country, and as smitten with the Selway as I am. I note early on in the hunt that he bugles infrequently, less than two or three times each morning. Opinions vary widely on elk calling, and my approach is always an aggressive one. Rather than being timid, I prefer to sound off regularly, but not to a point where it's overdone.

It's frustrating when we walk or ride through prime country and don't bugle, but I say nothing out of respect to my guide. Given my druthers, I'd be hunting on my own without a guide, but that's not always possible when one hunts a lot of places, and many of them unfamiliar.

I can stand it no longer when we slip through heavy forest that breaks away into a fairly open stand of lodgepole pine and I see three deeply gashed saplings. I know the slender trees were

These hunters team up. One calls while the other tries to spot the bull.

rubbed by a rut-crazed bull, and I sense that we're in the bull's back yard. It is the perfect place to make a call, yet my guide continues on.

Resorting to a bit of trickery, I ask my guide to pose for my camera next to a rather photogenic snag that sprouts orange and yellow branches. I ask him to put the bugle up next to his mouth, and he does so, but he doesn't blow into the call. I request that he belt out a bugle so his cheeks will be properly puffed up for an authentic photo. He does this too, and what happens next is a memory that will never dim in my mind.

A maddening scream tears out of the timber just 75 yards away, and I quickly dive for my rifle which I had put down in order to take the photos. The bull roars straight at us, so close I see his red nostrils flaring and urine dribbling onto the forest floor as he looks for us. He cocks his head excitedly, opens his mouth, and rips off another lusty bugle, followed by whines and grunts. He is mad, outraged that another bull should enter his domain.

Moments later, my .30/06 cracks. The bull runs 60 yards and falls to the ground. He is a lovely animal, with impressive six-point antlers that will score 320 B&C points.

If you don't get a response from a ridgetop like this, move down into the timber where other hunters are less likely to go.

A valuable lesson is learned here. My guide called into this drainage a half hour earlier. We were on the ridge, the air was calm, and the bull was within easy hearing distance, yet he did not respond.

PENETRATE HIS BACK YARD

During the breeding season, bulls set up territories often marked by rubs. As demonstrated during the hunt I mentioned above, a bull commonly ignores calls unless they're made from a location very close to or within his territory. Here is where many hunters err. It's easy to call from trails, along roadways, or other accessible places. Elk may fail to respond because they're alerted to those human traffic patterns, or simply because the caller poses no threat to the bull's lair.

A bull's territory isn't necessarily a certain patch of landscape that he never leaves. It may be wherever he happens to be at that particular moment you enter his world. Solo bulls often rove about, seeking cows, and herd bulls may drift along with their harem. In either case, I've found that bulls seem to draw the line at about 200 yards. If you get within that magic circle, odds are good that you'll draw in an irate customer.

If you don't call much, you run the obvious risk of walking by a bull that would otherwise have responded had you called. On the other hand, if you have plenty of company from other hunters, too much calling may work against you. Bulls hear the excessive vocalization, and if they associate the bugling with humans, you can practically insure the quarry's negative response. If you're in the woods and hear other "human" bugling, try blowing a cow call softly. Of course, be aware that other hunters may hear your calls and come looking for you. And vice versa. Don't think that a bad sounding call is always another hunter, by the way. Some of the worst sounding calls I've heard were made by real bulls, and not by people, as I first assumed. Use good judgment when other hunters are about, and always wear orange if you're hunting with a firearm, even if the state you're hunting in doesn't require it.

Calling is most effective at the edges of shooting light in the morning and afternoon. Be deep in the woods, and as far away from other hunters as you can get, even if this means traveling in the dark.

UNDERSTAND CALLING BASICS

Modern calls are simple to master, but don't assume you must be a world champion caller to lure in a bull. Learn the basics of blowing both bugle and cow calls by renting one of the many videos on the subject. Most large sporting goods stores have wide selections of videos. If you can blow the diaphragm call (a latex horseshoe-shaped call that fits entirely in your mouth) you're in business, but these calls are difficult to use, and many hunters can't blow them since they often produce a gagging reflex. There are many other types of calls that are far easier to blow. Some of the best elk hunters I know still use the old fashioned stiff "pipe" bugles that sound inferior to modern calls, but still work. I'm a firm believer that using a mediocre call and knowing how to react to a bull is far more important than knowing how to make the perfect call, but having no earthly idea what to do when the bull responds. I know some champion elk callers who win bugling contests but are poor hunters because they don't understand elk behavior.

Perhaps the most exasperating aspect of elk hunting is the standoff, a checkmate where neither side moves. Here's the scenario as it plays out. You get a response from a bull, and he approaches your location but hangs up. Your bugle calls are answered with eager responses, but he won't budge. This is often caused by a bull's reluctance to make the final commitment to enter your space. To do so invites a serious challenge. Some hunters believe this happens because the bull knows you're there. I don't believe it. If the bull knows you're there, he's history, and wastes no time heading over the back ridge.

To tempt this bull closer, you need to play some brain games. Stay silent for 10 or 15 minutes, and then softly blow a cow call. Make no more bugle sounds, but continue the cow calling. Be ever watchful, because this bull may sneak in silently. He's already heard you bugle, and now he hears only a cow. Because he doesn't know if a bull is present any longer, he's apt to slip in for a cautious look.

Another strategy is to try the "I'm tougher than you" routine. Break a branch with a loud snap and rake it noisily against a tree. Grab a nearby sapling and shake it hard. Bugle as you're going through these antics, telling the bull you're the meanest SOB in the valley. Again, be aware that he may come in quietly, but in this

Vin Sparano, former editor of Outdoor Life, calls for his son, Matt. They've moved rapidly through the dense woods, closing in on a stubborn bull that refused to approach.

case he's more apt to rush in with great verve and hostility. For this to work, you must be dealing with a bull that's in a mean mood. If he's in an intimidated mood, you'll run him off, but that's the chance you take. Bulls go through many mood stages, depending on their current standing in the woods.

Some bulls refuse to come to any ruse. I once messed with a bull for a week, trying every trick and approach known to man. I called him "Old Whistler", who lived in a dense blowdown in the midst of a spruce forest. He wouldn't leave his hideout, no matter how closely I approached. At one point I slipped into the blowdown, using the sweetest cow call you ever heard, but still no dice. I think this was an old bull who had seen it all, and was no longer interested in fighting or romancing. Perhaps he just wanted to live out his days in peace.

If you've been there and done that, you'll know how frustrating it is to talk to a bull, only to have him run away for apparently no reason. Your initial reaction is to blame yourself, assuming you're making bad calls or that the bull is wise to you. Not necessarily so. There are two types of bulls you'll be dealing with, and each has a perfectly natural reason to run away.

The first type is a herd bull. He's already gathered a harem of cows, and his primary objective in life is to keep them in his possession until he breeds them all. Many forces are at work to foil this scenario. The bull must sometimes keep his cows rounded up by brandishing his antlers, and rushing cows who decide to simply walk away and leave his little love nest. A cow may walk off because she either wants out of the party and doesn't care much for the host, or she hears another bull who sounds more interesting. Then, of course, the herd bull must deal with other bulls who want to share his prizes. If he's an aggressive bull, he may streak out to challenge an intruder bull by either outbluffing him or actually making physical contact. If he's insecure in his hierarchy in the woods and somewhat intimidated, he may run his cows off, away from the bugling challenger.

So there you are, blowing your world-class bugle call flawlessly, just like the experts do, but your dream bull is running away from you. Take heart in realizing that even a *live* bull cannot turn this fleeing bull, and think romance instead of war. Put the bugle call away and begin a sweet melody of cow chirps. Be ready for action, because your chicken-hearted bull may suddenly stop in his tracks, leave his cows momentarily, and rush down to check out the newest lady elk in the woods.

The second type of bull is a solo bull. Some hunters refer to him as a satellite or a raghorn bull, a youngster who wears four or five points to the side and is no match for the harem master. This is the usual case, but some solo bulls may be old-timers who own impressive racks but are no longer physically able to compete with stronger, dominant bulls. Loner bulls have one thing in common. They have no cows, and are unhappy with that lot in life. If they hear another bugle, chances are they won't respond in aggressive fashion. They may bugle back, but that's it, or they may sneak in to see if any loose cows are with the bull they hear, taking pains to stay a safe distance away. Most commonly, they'll retreat. As subdominant bulls, they don't want the risk of clashing with Mr. Big. The same holds for the overmature solo bull. He's also unwilling to skirmish.

The solution? Use the cow call. Logic tells you that single bulls want company. Make them think you're what they're seeking. I'm such a firm believer in the cow call that I seldom use a bugle call at all. For me, the cow call does it all.

Elk are polygamous animals, as are all other members of the deer family, but unlike buck deer, bulls are in constant contact with females, never letting them out of their sight during the breeding season. Keeping the cows in a tight herd is a 24 hour a day job, and bulls are constantly trying to either retain the cows they have or are attempting to win more. By September 20 or so, the rut reaches a frenzy, with bulls tearing about wildly, looking for cows. Much activity occurs between bulls as they establish dominance. Most commonly, two bulls will approach each other, bugle wildly, and demolish saplings with their antlers. The bluffing match continues until one of the bulls runs off. Antler sparring is the ultimate challenge, and may last several minutes. This is no lightweight shoving contest. It's a duel to the death, with 700 pound bodies savaging each other amidst a great deal of noise, dust, and sometimes, plenty of blood. It's not unusual for a bull to kill an adversary.

No matter how good a caller you are, you might not be able to entice a herd bull away from his cows.

Much of this activity occurs at night. Bugling itself may be suppressed by weather, such as damp, rainy periods, or during exceptionally hot weather. If bugling becomes infrequent or nonexistent, don't believe that breeding has stopped. Not at all. It contin-

ues, even though vocalization halts. Continue calling as usual, but expect silent approaches by responding bulls.

As the breeding season winds down in early October, well established harems begin breaking up, and bulls focus in on cows that haven't yet been bred. Although activity isn't as hectic as during the peak of the season, bulls are still very much in breeding mode, and will continue to respond. If you hear bugling in late October or even November or December, you're probably hearing a bull sounding off at a cow that wasn't bred during the rut, but has come back in heat again. These bulls seldom respond to calling.

I mentioned this elsewhere in the book, but I'll repeat it because it's so important: *Blow your cow call to stop a spooked elk.*

This amazing technique works like a charm. All it takes is a cow call and the confidence that it works. When an elk, or herd of elk, is running away, blow your cow call sharply, as loud as you can. Be prepared for a shot, because the elk are likely to stop and look back at you. Wear your call around your neck so it's handy when you need it. Trust me, this strategy is remarkably effective. Most hunters haven't tried it because the last thing you do when elk are fleeing is to think to blow a call. Instead, you're jockeying for a shot. Be a believer and blow the call.

Why does it work? My best guess is that it somewhat imitates the bark of a spooked cow. A bark is a warning—she's alerted to something she doesn't like. When a cow barks, the other elk stop what they're doing and stare at the cow. They stay rooted to the spot, until one of them takes off. Then the rest follow, or they mill around for a moment or two until they decide which way they want to go.

Like I say, this is my best guess, but for whatever reason, the trick works incredibly well.

Chapter 16

In the Trenches for Elk

The conditions couldn't have been worse for elk hunting. The temperature was 80 degrees, and the hot sun beat mercilessly through cloudless skies. It was great weather for golfing, swimming, or fishing, but elk hunters were having a tough time of it, every one of us wishing desperately for a change. Snow would have been a godsend, but the forecast called for more balmy, hot days.

Though the elk woods were lovely, it was an awful state of affairs in the forest, at least as far as hunting goes. Elk were "jungled-up" as we like to say during periods of very hot weather, sulking in cool hideaways deep in the recesses of tilted land. They were as elusive as they get.

The timing added to our woes. It was mid-October, when the general season was in full swing, during a period I call the transition stage. Hunters were everywhere, pushing elk into tough security cover. Breeding was over, so bugling was out. It was too early for the migrations that would begin when the snows came, so the elk were everywhere in their vast domain—many of them in remote or hard to reach spots. You could lay a safe wager that most would be a good distance from a road or well-used trail.

And there you had it—silent, sulking, spooky elk, tucked away in miserable patches of timber. It was bad news, and I knew that very few of the hunters sharing the mountain with me would see an elk, much less get one.

This scenario is common in the October woods. Some years the snow comes early, but too often it disappears quickly, and the balmy weather reestablishes itself. Novice hunters begin to understand why only 25 percent of all elk hunters are successful each year. Most will go home with unpunched tags.

Is there a way to beat the dismal odds of scoring during spells of hot, dry weather? Yes, and no, depending on what kind of shape you're in, how hard you're willing to work, your knowledge of elk behavior, and your skills in the woods. You could, of course, be lucky and shoot an elk within sight of camp, but don't count on it. Prepare for the worst, and don't forget the awesome task of getting your elk out of the woods. It's likely that your warm-weather elk will fall in a spot far from a road. This is the one time when your hunt will most definitely not be easy.

To be successful, one basic consideration outweighs every other. You must hunt where elk exist. This might seem to be a simple, fundamental rule that needs no discussion, but you'd be surprised how many hunters pursue elk where there are no elk. That's where knowledge of elk habits and behavior comes in. You must know what to look for and where to look.

Being social animals, elk live in herds. The bunch of animals you're hoping to find might be several mountains away. Elk have a huge home range, up to 25 square miles and more, and you could hunt for a week and never be within a half mile of a herd. Long before you begin your hunt you should set up the planning process, determining areas inhabited by good populations of elk.

Having established the "where" -- your next move is to formulate a game plan. With an updated map in hand (all public agencies sell maps for a modest fee, usually less than $5), you should become thoroughly acquainted with the hunting unit. Try to arrive a couple days early to scout. I've found that a very small number of hunters ever scout prior to the season, primarily because they don't have time. Remember that in the public woods full of hunters, competition is keen. Astute hunters will take advantage of every opportunity.

If you see elk prior to the season grazing in meadows and clearcuts, always assume that other hunters have spotted them too. It's frustrating to have a bunch of elk located, only to have someone else beat you to them on opening day. Do your best on opening morning to get to those animals first, but if you don't

When elk are in the timber, they may be difficult to locate. These hunters look for animals as soon as it's light enough to see in the morning.

score, write that spot off for the rest of the season. If you or other hunters spook the elk, be assured they'll quickly move into security cover, and stay there until hunter pressure lets up. It's a brand new game, and that's when you need to go to the trenches. Hunters waste thousands of hours each fall as they wait in vain for elk to show up because they saw a herd in that spot before the season opened. All the hunters get is some rest.

The biggest mistake most hunters make during hot spells when hunter pressure is heavy is to watch openings and meadows during

midday hours. If you do that, you might as well bring along a book to read. You won't accomplish much else, and certainly won't see any elk.

Confine your observation of meadows to only during the first and last minutes of the day, because that's when elk will be there, if at all. Most animals will feed under cover of darkness, but you might catch elk leaving the meadows in the morning just at the edge of shooting hours. The same holds true at night. Stay until shooting hours are over.

After the rut is over, elk play hide and seek in the timber. Note how difficult it is to spot this bull.

My strategy in crowded woods is to get as high as I can, where a lofty vantage point gives me a wide field of view below. To do this, I travel in the night, using a flashlight only when necessary, and taking advantage of light from stars and the moon. A map and pencil are always part of my equipment, and in fact are essential to this strategy. Before heading out, I want to know the location of all roads and major trails. It's a good idea to learn where most of the competition from other hunters will come from.

With luck, I'll spot elk in the dim light of the new morning. If they're close enough to make a stalk, I'll immediately head out, using the wind correctly and hoping to ambush them before they drift back in the timber. If the elk are too far to get to, I'll mark the

location of the meadow they're in on my map. If this seems to be a waste of time, consider that the landscape has an amazing way of changing as you move through timber. The clearing that was so obvious to you from your vantage spot may be out of sight from your new location, or it might look entirely different. You won't be the first one to scratch your head and try to figure out where that seemingly obvious piece of land disappeared to. It's also possible that a number of clearings are in the area, and you'll want to know precisely which one held the elk.

The idea here is to intercept the elk as they come back out of the timber in the evening. If not disturbed, they'll likely use the same route they traveled in the morning. Of course, you need to be able to find your way out of the forest in dim light that evening, which is the second reason the map will be handy. As you work your way to the clearing, plan a route that you'll take out after shooting light is over. If no trails or forest roads are available, use well-defined natural features that are easily followed in poor light, such as ridgetops and creeks.

There's always a temptation to hunt the woods where the elk entered in the morning, hoping to catch them bedded. First, be aware that even though the timber is thick, elk may walk a mile or more to a bedding spot. They seldom lay up close to the meadow where they're feeding. I'll stay away from the general area because there's a high risk of spooking the animals and being unable to get a shot. Better to avoid the place and take a stand later on near the clearing, hoping they'll show up before dark. I'll look for them in the timber only if I have no other days to hunt or I have to be out of the woods early.

Let's say you've seen no elk, but your scouting shows plenty of fresh sign. What you have is a bunch of nocturnal animals that never show themselves by day. This is frequently the case in heavy-pressure woods during hot weather. Your best option is to penetrate the timber, looking for bedded animals. Of course, you'll be hunting blind, counting on stumbling into the quarry. Once you spot fresh sign, you can slow down and start stillhunting.

You can increase your odds of finding elk by heading for north facing spruce-fir slopes. I've found that elk like to bed under a ridgeline on slopes of 25 to 35 degrees of angle. Heavy blowdowns are no deterrent to elk, and provide excellent security cover, but you'll find yourself hard-pressed to move

quietly. In that case, I blow a cow call frequently, reassuring bedded elk that I'm one of their own kind, allowing me to get closer.

Spruce and fir trees seem to be attractive to elk, possibly because they grow thick, their branches reach to the ground, and they offer cool screening cover. These are also climax species, being the last in the chain of progressional changes in the timber's composition, and also known as old-age or virgin forests. While producing little food because of the tight canopy that prevents the sun from hitting the ground, these are the busted, windblown forests so attractive to elk looking for a hideout. These forests grow at the higher locations of the Rockies from New Mexico to Canada. To identify a spruce, look for trees with thick branches having short needles about one-inch long. Carefully squeeze your palm around a cluster of needles. If it feels like you're holding a needle-sharp cactus branch, you're in touch with a spruce. Firs will be nearby, growing in close association with spruce trees. Technically, the spruce of the Rockies is the Englemann spruce, firs are typically alpine firs. If your elk hunting country is along the Cascade or coastal region of Oregon and Washington, you'll be dealing with at least a half dozen firs and a variety of other evergreen species. Elk are much more scattered in those forests, and can be anywhere.

During dry weather, elk will key on water holes, but in country with plenty of creeks you won't have any idea where they're watering since they drink randomly from different locations. In forests that have sparse water sources, elk will seek out springs and seeps. You can often locate those by looking for betraying patches of lush green foliage on timbered slopes. Quite often, alder and other water-loving shrubs will grow around a spring. Their leaves are a different green from the surrounding forest and are often easily discerned. Be sure to accurately pinpoint the spring on your map. If you spotted it in the distance, you may never find it again unless you have a solid reference.

Making crowds work for you can be an effective strategy, though this is admittedly a hit or miss proposition, since you have no control of human movements. Give me a hot, dry forest in October and a choice of woods with few hunters or woods with plenty of hunters, and I'll opt for the latter. I've taken a number of bulls stirred up by other people.

Jim Zumbo glasses just before the sun goes down, looking for elk coming out of the timber to feed.

To make this work, place yourself in or along an escape route leading to or from security cover. My hands-down choice of an escape route is a saddle on a ridgetop. You can make good money by wagering that practically every elk in a drainage will exit via a saddle. A saddle is nothing more than a well-defined dip or depression on a ridgetop. Ridges with many saddles may give you too many choices—if that's the case, look for trails and fresh tracks. A vegetated saddle is even better.

Jim Zumbo with a bull he took in a jungle. Hunting elk in the timber is definitely not the easiest way to do it.

For years I hunted a thickly timbered drainage either alone or with a buddy. Early on I discovered a saddle well-used by elk, and I never saw it fail on weekends or around the opener when plenty of people were in the woods. I had a special spot near a trio of aspen trees that allowed me to see most of the saddle. Few other hunters climbed up the ridge because it was an arduous hike across some nasty rockslides. Sometimes only cows and calves or spike bulls showed up, but at least I was seeing elk, and it was consistent. Most other hunters were seeing no elk, and this was in an area that gave up a dismal 10 percent hunter success rate.

Try to be flexible. If you've been hunting for several days and are seeing no elk and little fresh sign, there's a temptation to try another spot. That's not a bad idea, but your decision is really a roll of the dice. Sometimes it's best to stay with a spot that you're familiar with and stick it out. Often elk are pushed into areas from other drainages by hunters; your seemingly barren area could come alive with elk. On the other hand, trying new country might motivate you to hunt harder and longer. If you want to beat the odds, you'll need to work at it. Always bear in mind that elk country can be unforgiving. Being savvy and wise to the quarry's behavior might work in the whitetail woods, but elk country has the added dimension of a physical workout. And that, I'm afraid, is the bottom line. There are few shortcuts; which, translated, means that elk hunting is very often not easy.

Jim Zumbo with a nice Idaho bull that lived in a very thick lodgepole pine forest. Elk will hide out in areas like this when hunters are about.

Colorado offers three hunts. Author took this bull that moved out of the high country.

Chapter 17

Go Late for an Easy Elk

Show me a hunter who waits for the last few days of elk season to head for the woods, and I'll show you a person who hunts smart. He may freeze half to death, and wallow in snow up to his butt, but at least his suffering is apt to lead him to an elk, and probably an easier one than if he'd been hunting early in the season.

Why is this so? Elsewhere in this book you've read about elk migrations. When snow piles high, they head to lower elevations where they're more concentrated. It's important to remember this basic fact: elk essentially live in two places—a summer range and winter range. Summer range is the high country where they're scattered everywhere, up to and higher than timberline. Winter range is a tiny sliver of their entire home range, usually where there are roads and the landscape isn't so steep. Add it all up, and you can easily see where playing the waiting game has plenty of advantages. But bundle up and wear a warm hat.

Here's an account of an elk hunt my wife, Madonna, experienced recently. I'll never forget it, and neither will she.

It was the kind of morning best spent indoors around a cozy fireplace. A ripping 50 mile per hour gale drove stinging crystals of snow into my face, and the 10 below zero temperature added to

the misery. My wife, Madonna, wasn't enjoying the arctic conditions any more than I, but she wasn't complaining. We were hot on the heels of a big bull elk, and she had a Wyoming elk tag in her pocket. Pain and suffering were acceptable.

Madonna had drawn a precious late elk tag, one that allowed her to hunt long after the general October season. She had the last two weeks of November and the first week of December to collect a bull. While the late tag wasn't a guarantee, it was close to it. The weather had cooperated nicely, and plenty of elk were in the lower elevations.

Our strategy was to hike up a different canyon each day, walk as far as time allowed, and get back to the truck at dark. Because I had other hunts in November, we waited for the last week to try for her bull. The late elk season would close December 7th, and I figured the last few days would be best, since elk were still moving steadily out of the high country. All our hunting would be on public land in the Shoshone National Forest which borders Yellowstone Park. Our home is just a few hundred yards below the forest boundary, and we commonly spotted elk from our house. I wasn't terribly concerned about her tagging a bull, the question was: how big?

We saw plenty of elk the first couple of days, some as soon as we left the pickup. But this was big bull country, with plenty of animals coming out of the famed Thorofare wilderness region as well as Yellowstone Park. Madonna intended on holding out for a bruiser.

Practically every canyon has a horse trail in the bottom. We'd strike up the trail, hike several miles in; then we'd leave it and start climbing the very steep slopes. Though there were several feet of snow in the higher elevations, only a few inches blanketed the lower regions, which is exactly why the elk were down.

It was tough going, with plenty of slipping and sliding. At places we needed walking sticks to maintain our balance and allow us to get a good boot grip. The snow was very cold, which made it loud and squeaky. Trying to get close to elk was a challenge. Most of the animals we'd seen were a half mile away or more. Many were on the lee of the slopes, where they were protected from the fierce winds that blew every day.

I was curious about one particular canyon that I'd never been up before, and called an outfitter buddy who had been in the area.

"I wouldn't get very far back in there," he said. "The trail goes in only five miles, and then it's no man's land."

"Why do you call it that?" I asked.

"No trails anywhere," he said. "Can't get a horse around, and it's a miserable tangle of timber that's full of grizzlies in the summer."

I had to chuckle at my pals words. A typical westerner, he wasn't about to go where his horse wouldn't take him. That's fairly typical for some folks who like horseflesh between their legs as much as possible. As it was, that horseflesh would be most welcome if Madonna killed a bull off in the boonies. My plan was to bone it and backpack the meat down to a trail where I'd borrow a couple horses from neighbors. And the grizzlies, of course, wouldn't be a problem. They'd be denned up.

Author with a Montana bull he took during the latter part of the season. This bull probably migrated out of Yellowstone Park.

We hiked into no man's land, and had tough going where the trail merged with a creek. In places, the vertical canyon sidewalls required us to gingerly walk on a thin shell of ice that covered the shallow creek. Falling through was a regular event, but the water was only a few inches deep. Nonetheless, it made for very noisy travel, and fresh elk tracks in the bottom encouraged silent walking.

We covered about four miles and were paying more attention to walking on the thin ice than to our surroundings. That's when I looked ahead and gasped in shock when I saw a big bull standing in the bottom, drinking from where he'd busted a hole in the ice. The bull saw me at the same time I saw him, and he reacted by wheeling and charging into the timber. Madonna had no time for a shot.

I saw flashes of elk hide as the bull tore through the timber, and told Madonna to get ready. A small open bluff on the slope was in his path, and he might stop to look.

He did, but so briefly that my wife didn't have time to get a solid rest. The elk was out there at about 250 yards, and she wasn't about to try a shot from an unsteady rest. That was it. The bull was history, though we followed him for two hours into unforgiving patches of timber and very steep slopes. Early on we saw in the snow where he had previously bedded with nine other very large elk, presumably all bulls by the size of the beds. Eventually the tracks mixed with others, and we came to places so heavily marked with prints that it was impossible to follow a single set of tracks. I judged that at least a hundred elk shared the mountainside with us, all of them heading in different directions.

While eating lunch that day, on a ridge in the middle of no man's land, an average five point bull walked within 10 yards of us. Having seen the very big six pointer and knowing the quality of other bulls in the area, Madonna let him walk. Wise choice. Getting chunks of elk meat off the mountain to the trail far below might have been all downhill, but in places you'd need repelling ropes and maybe a hang glider.

Two days later, while carefully negotiating a razorback ridge, Madonna found a horseshoe. It was truly in the middle of nowhere, and she suggested it might bring us luck. Presently we came upon a trail, with a pair of fresh horse tracks on it. Madonna had just admitted that she wasn't looking forward to sliding and falling back down the mountain when we were ready to leave the ridge, which was the routine every day, so I suggested we backtrack on the horse prints. They were made that morning, and they had to take us back to the road, hopefully along a trail even though there weren't supposed to be any trails.

After an hour of following, and about half way back to the road, the tracks told a new story. There was sort of skirmish on the

ridge, and the horses now led back down into a thick blowdown along a creek. Then the tracks split up, and we followed one track. Soon we encountered a horse, bloody and beat, standing in a tangle that evidently trapped him. He wore a halter and a torn up pack saddle that was about to fall off. His lunging and thrashing allowed him to bust branches and stand free, and he wasn't terribly excited about seeing us. Though he tried to kick my teeth out, I managed to calm him and led him the last couple miles down the road. We found his owner later that evening.

This is a common sight in Gardiner, Montana, which is adjacent to Yellowstone Park. Many elk are taken as they migrate out of the park, provided snow conditions are right.

A neighbor called that night and told us where he'd seen a big bull not far from our house. Madonna and I were in the area before shooting light the next morning, and waited in the screaming wind for daylight. Having hunted in the north all my life, I can't remember being much colder.

It was just breaking day when we saw a big bull running down a steep slope 90 yards away. I blew my cow call sharply, and the elk skidded to a halt and looked at us. The Browning 7mm Mag roared instantly and the bull staggered from a solid hit. He made a leap and started down the mountain, but Madonna drilled him

once more, anchoring him for good. Both shots were in the lungs; a baseball would cover the bullet holes.

I couldn't believe it when we walked up to the grand bull. Everything happened so fast I didn't have a chance to count points, but when you see a bull with the kind of rack this one had, you don't count. A big bull *looks* big. It was with a whole lot of astonishment that I stared at the antlers. This incredible elk had only five points to the side. The main beams were long and extremely massive, with thick impressive tines. In all my years of elk hunting, I had never seen a five pointer with this kind of unbelievable mass and length, and neither had the veteran elk hunters who saw it later and the taxidermist who mounted the elk afterward. I was most happy with this bull because it would make a great conversation piece and was so unusual. If it indeed had carried six points, it would still have been a great bull, but not as noteworthy. Madonna didn't care how many points it had. She was a happy lady.

On another delightful note, the bull fell near a road, and I had him quartered and hanging in the garage by noon. That, as the old saying goes, is a good elk.

To a late season elk hunter, good weather means lots of snow—enough to drive animals from their high country haunts and down onto winter ranges. Since elk are grazers and depend on grass much of the year, they have no choice when deep snow covers their food. Either they starve or leave the upper elevations. No contest—they leave.

Sometimes conditions are right but the hunt doesn't work out. A couple weeks before Madonna got her elk, I hunted in Montana at outfitter Max Chase's place north of Yellowstone Park with Jack Atcheson Jr., a hunter's booking agent from nearby Butte. Max's hunters pick off bulls coming out of the park, and the hunting is best when the snow is deepest.

We got word that a couple hundred bulls were headed our way. Knowing the stature of some of these Yellowstone elk, Jack and I passed on several small bulls and bided our time. The weather was bitterly cold, with high winds and low temperatures, just right to keep elk on the move.

As bad luck would have it, the weather moderated. A warm Chinook wind blew in, and the temperature rose from zero to 50 degrees. Snow melted quickly, and frozen trails were soon

Author's wife, Madonna Zumbo, glasses for elk during the late season. She drew a tag that allowed her to hunt migrating animals.

replaced by mud. More word about the migrating elk filtered in, and it wasn't good. The animals had holed up somewhere in the vast timbered slopes somewhere between us and the park. We continued to see bulls, and other members in our party filled their tags, but Jack and I held out for the big boys.

One evening, while riding horseback to camp after a long day hunting, Jack looked up and saw a huge bull in the dim light. It was too late to make a stalk, but we tried in the morning. Tracks in the snow showed a total of 11 bulls, and though we followed, they led up into a mountain that had melted off, and plenty of other tracks in the dirt mingled with those of the bulls, and we never caught up.

Jack and I went home without bulls. As a matter of interest, another of Max's hunters took the big bull after we left. He had a distinctive broken tine, and there was no question. The elk scored around 330 B&C.

Several years before, Jack's Dad, Jack Atcheson Sr. and I hunted the same region. No stranger to OUTDOOR LIFE readers, Jack Sr. guided Jack O'Connor on many hunts, as well as accompanying Jim Carmichel and myself on a number of other hunts. Jim and I like to write about Jack, because he's a superb hunter and a

great guy to share a campfire with.

On this occasion, Jack and I were hunting during the last week of Montana's season, basing out of a cabin owned by one of Jack's hunting buddies. We hadn't yet gotten into any bulls when Gary Duffy, a local outfitter and friend of Jack's, showed up and invited us to hunt some of his country.

Two mornings later, after hiking up onto a knob in Gary's hunting area that afforded good visibility, I was beginning to believe that I was slowly freezing to death in the 30 below zero temperature. Then three huge bulls appeared below me. It was all I could do to rip off my mittens, and when I finally shucked them I tagged the biggest bull. He is one of my best ever, scoring 343 B&C.

What happens when the weather is mild and the elk don't show? Quite often, nothing happens. Except for resident elk that live in the area year around, some of those hunts go bust in a big way. Obviously, you can't shoot what doesn't exist. Therefore, a whole lot of praying goes on by outfitters and hunters alike for snow, lots of it.

Why hunt late when you can call a big bull during the mild September rutting season? First, if you're a rifle hunter, most states have general firearms seasons after the rut is over. Unless you hunt with a bow, or hunt some backcountry early gun seasons, you can't pursue elk in the rut. Second, the biggest herd bulls often don't respond to your calls (see the chapter—The Basics of Calling).

Elk, even the biggest bulls, do not have a choice when winter approaches. They come down where they're more accessible, and more easily seen in the snow. Tracks betray their movements as well.

My advice is to hunt as late as possible if you want to beat the odds. Colorado, for example, has three elk seasons. I always choose the last one. Montana's five week season traditionally runs to Sunday of Thanksgiving week. I'll always opt for the last few days. And so on with other states.

And, from what my wife, Madonna, accomplished during a late hunt, you can bet we'll keep on applying for those special late tags offered in lottery draws. Most states have them. If you win a tag, you won't be awarded a bunch of money as in a state lottery, but you'll win a chance at a bull of a lifetime. That's plenty of reason to keep applying. Don't be surprised if your elk turns out to be an easy one.

CHAPTER 18

HUNTING STRATEGIES THAT WORK

Every species has unique characteristics requiring strategies that fit with the quarry's behavior. In the case of elk, bugling and cow calling allow some very special techniques not possible with other big game species. This chapter is intended to present hunting scenarios, including all possible factors that may affect an elk's response. After considering all the information for each scenario, I've offered a number of options.

It's necessary to understand that every confrontation in the elk woods is different. What works in one situation might not work in another. Elk are unpredictable, so it's important to try various methods if the first one fails.

There's a very important calling strategy that is so consistently effective that I'm going to address it again, even though I've done so elsewhere in this book. That is—at every opportunity, when nothing else seems to work, be *aggressive*. The biggest error made by hunters is being too timid. Many people, including some good outfitters and guides I've known, bugle too infrequently. Additionally, plenty of hunters will listen to a bull retreat, assuming the hunter has made a mistake, or his calling is poor. As a result, he shakes his head, figures the bull is too wary, and heads for a new spot.

That's a mistake. Assume that every bull is callable, no matter what he does. Of course, if he bugles consistently enough that you hear him go over a ridge, it's time for a new option, perhaps with another bull.

Using binoculars frequently is a key to locating animals. There's no such thing as glassing too much.

So how do you be aggressive? First, *do* call frequently. If the wind is blowing or you're hunting near a noisy creek or in heavy timber, call every five minutes or so. Another aggressive technique, as I've explained before, and I'll do it again, because it's so *very* important, is to quit calling from trails, roads, and ridgetops. Get down there where the elk are! Cross the stream, hike up the other mountain, wander around canyon bottoms. Try every place that an elk might be hiding, and that will be precisely where other hunters don't go.

Aggressiveness also means literally running at the bull, even at a fast trot, if required. Depending on the circumstances, you can

bugle as you run, use the cow call, or scrape a branch against the bark of a tree, simulating another bull. Don't be afraid to make plenty of noise as you run, but avoid human or metallic noises. Break branches, shake sapling trees, make as many natural sounds as you can. Of course, consider the wind direction as you approach.

When you call, always be prepared for an immediate reaction from an elk. Don't call from an area where you can't get a shot if you're a bowhunter. Don't lean your rifle against a tree. Have it ready—you'll never know when the quarry will show up.

When choosing a calling location, find a spot where you have fair visibility, but don't overdo it. Don't set up at the edge of a big meadow. Few bulls will cross a large opening, especially where there is other hunter activity. You might get away with it in wilderness areas or limited entry units.

By all means, be out there in the woods long before daylight. You might hear the bulk of the vocalization for the day prior to shooting light. You might not be able to see the animals, but at least you can mark their locations, and try them later.

Most vocalizing will occur early in the morning and late in the afternoon. Make every effort to be in prime elk country during that time. Most hunters aren't very excited about walking out of the woods in the dark, but you should strongly consider it if you're really serious about your hunting. Obviously, make sure that you can find your way out in the night, by hunting near a trail, waterway, or other path.

Here are a number of different situations that you might encounter. My options are merely logical strategies based on past experience, common sense, and, above all, hopeful guesstimates.

Yes, you'll do lots of guessing. There's no exact science when it comes to hunting. *Do* dare to be different. Some of the wildest things have happened to me when I tried something strange. You'll never know unless you try it. Above all, don't use traditional techniques exclusively if they don't work. Elk are unique animals. You should be unique as well.

Though I could have listed dozens of possible situations, I didn't because too many would be confusing. Instead, I've come up with a few, all of which I've tried. Basically I've attempted here to merely illustrate the need to be different, to try various techniques and to use the cow call as well as the bugle call.

SITUATION #1

DATE: August 25
WEATHER: very hot and dry—temperatures reach a daytime high of 80 and a low of 50 in the evenings.
VEGETATION: quaking aspen, with Douglas fir on northern slopes at ends of ridges, thick stands of oak brush on some southern exposures, plenty of grass in aspen stands and brushy slopes.
TOPOGRAPHY: mountainous, with moderate canyons and fairly gentle slopes.
HUNTING PRESSURE: light, only a few hunters.
ROAD ACCESS: Roads are plentiful. Most major canyons and ridges are roaded.
GENERAL DESCRIPTION: It's bow season, and elk are not vocalizing. You've seen elk early in the morning and late in the afternoon feeding in the distance, but they don't respond to bull or cow calls. They seem to be whimsical, not adhering to any definite patterns. You suspect they're "timbered-up" because of the hot weather.

OPTION #1: If you've been listening during the early morning, late afternoon, and even during the night and hear no bugling, it's reasonable to assume that elk aren't vocalizing. They should be preparing for the breeding season however, and that plus the hot weather should attract them to wallows.

Look for wallows around beaver marshes if any are present, or along sidehills, especially where there is a patch of lush vegetation. If cattle trails are in the area, follow them, because they often lead to waterholes.

If you find a fresh wallow with rubbed trees in the vicinity, try watching it from a ground blind or tree stand. If nothing happens over the course of a couple days, try bugling and/or cow calling. It's possible that a bull might be visiting the wallow at night, and is bedded close by. Your calling could bring him in.

OPTION #2: Since it's bow season, you don't have much of an option other than watching wallows or calling to attract an animal within bow range. However, you might try watching trails that you suspect elk are using. If you spot distant animals early in the morning, note which way they head for the timber when they're done feeding. Use a spotting scope or binoculars. By determining

their route, you can set up within bow range, and ambush the animals as they come out to feed in late afternoon. They'll often use the same trail as they travel to and from bedding areas.

Be prepared for bad weather when you hunt. Elk hunting is usually at its best when the weather is at its worst.

SITUATION #2

DATE: September 25
WEATHER: hot and dry—temperatures approach 80 each day, drop to 45 and 50 in the evenings.
VEGETATION: typical fir, spruce, and pine stands; meadows are scattered in the forest, basically composed of evergreens.
TOPOGRAPHY: steep mountains, typical for the Rockies; elevation is about 8,500 feet.
HUNTING PRESSURE: very light. A few hunters are in the same area, but competition from them is light or nonexistent.
ROAD ACCESS: little to none.

GENERAL DESCRIPTION: You're hunting an early rifle season during the prime bugle period. As such, you're in a limited entry unit or a backcountry area, both of which offer early seasons to rifle hunters. One morning, you bugle and receive a response within 300 yards. The bull seems interested, answering your call, but it appears to be a standoff. He stays where he is, and his calls become more infrequent. From the sound of his bugle, you have him pinpointed in a thicket on a steep sidehill above you.

A very slight breeze is blowing downhill, but you know that night and early morning thermals normally blow down slope. As the temperature heats up, however, the wind is apt to change, carrying your scent to the bull. You'll have to move fast.

OPTION #1: Quit calling for ten minutes, and walk up the slope at a diagonal, so your route will bring you just below the bull. Softly use the cow call, varying the pitch so you sound like more than one animal. Blow the cow call every two minutes or so, and don't be afraid to break a few small branches as you walk. The idea here is to make the bull think you're a herd of elk, with or without a bull. Remember, he heard you bugling, and now he hears only cows. He'll likely respond to your cow sounds by bugling at you. When he does, bugle back. Don't be surprised if he comes unglued and looks for you. If he doesn't answer, silently and quickly climb up the slope, making a wide berth of the bull's location. Watch the wind. When you feel you're 200 or 300 yards above the bull, try a bugle call. He might respond to you in your new location. If he does, but shows no inclination to approach, try the aggressive method. Rapidly move down slope, heading directly toward the bull. Stop every 30 or 40 yards, bugle and scrape a branch against a tree. Now you're simulating an agitated bull who's trying to pick a fight. Keep moving in, stopping every now and then, repeating the performance. Be alert, because this is one situation in which the bull might respond silently.

OPTION #2: Make a sudden attack on the bull from the beginning. As soon as you realize he isn't coming, charge straight up to his location, bugling and thrashing brush every 50 yards or so. If he remains silent, quit bugling, and try grunting, whining like a spoiled child. This often does the trick. He might not be able to stand your antics.

Be sure to be out of camp, looking for elk, before shooting light arrives. You may spot animals moving from feeding to bedding areas.

SITUATION # 3

Date and conditions are exactly the same as SITUATION #2.
GENERAL DESCRIPTION: Despite it being prime bugle time, the forests are absolutely silent. You can't believe it. Though you're out early in the morning and late in the afternoon, you don't hear a single bugle. It seems like there are no elk in the mountains you're hunting, though you see fresh tracks and plenty of rubbed trees. You know the elk are out there, but you can't locate them. It's a maddening situation, one that happens often in good elk country.

OPTION #1: Put your hiking boots on and head for the hills. It's time to find elk. First, consider the thickest blowdown country you can find. Walk through it, softly using the cow call every five minutes. It's impossible to be quiet, so you might as well sound like an elk. If you find a cluster of freshly rubbed trees, or three or four trees in a small area, use the bugle call. If there are any deep canyons without roads or trails in the bottoms, work down to the bottoms. You'll likely see plenty of sign, and you might find some

This is classic country for elk to bed in the daytime. Be sure to hunt the timber in places where other hunters may avoid.

wallows. Bugle frequently as you move through the bottom—every five minutes is okay, if there's a creek present and the timber is thick, as it usually is. It's amazing how the topography, vegetation, and stream noises will absorb or screen a bugle call. In places, your call might not carry more than 100 yards. You don't necessarily have to look into only remote spots. What you need to find is country undisturbed by hunters. Sometimes the most obvious places harbor bulls because hunters overlook them.

OPTION #2: Though the woods are silent, you can bet that elk are in the breeding mode. If they aren't vocalizing early and late in the day, they're probably bugling at night. Take a stroll from camp during the evening hours, listening intently. If you hear nothing, give a call with your bugle. Sometimes bulls will answer, even in the distance. If you get a response, don't bugle again. Since it's night you obviously don't want to call in a bull, just locate them. Night calling is a new approach, and hasn't really been well-tested. I've tried it a number of times, and it works consistently enough that I'm convinced it's an excellent strategy. After determining their location, hunt that spot intently the next day.

SITUATION #4

DATE: September 25
WEATHER: cool, sunny days—frosty in the mornings, highs in the 60's.
VEGETATION: Lodgepole pine, Douglas fir throughout, some meadows.
TOPOGRAPHY: steep, with a number of canyons running throughout.
HUNTING PRESSURE: very light.
ROAD ACCESS: few roads, most access is via foot or horseback.
GENERAL DESCRIPTION: This is an elk hunter's dream. Bulls are bugling everywhere in the mornings, but the hunt is turning into a nightmare. Regardless of what you do, you can't call in an elk. You try working two or three bulls each morning, and without failure they finally quit responding and fade away. You figure you're doing something very wrong, and wish you were a better caller.

Your calling probably isn't the reason you're getting no action. It's likely that you're hunting an area with a low bull to cow ratio. Each bull has a harem, and the herd bulls are quite content to stay with their harems and avoid a fight.

OPTION #1: Try the cow call if you haven't already. Avoid bugling, instead listening for a bull to bugle on his own. Approach his location as slowly as possible, and softly blow on the cow call. Keep it up, blowing every 10 minutes. Blow only once each time, but call lightly. Cows never call with any velocity. Be watchful for a silent bull. Often he'll come in without a peep. Possibly you'll have attracted a solo bull who hasn't rounded up a harem, and he'll sneak in quietly to try to claim the cow. He doesn't know if the cow is alone or with a herd bull, so he's apt to ease in to investigate.

OPTION #2: Try the aggressive route again. Charge after a bull who taunts you by merely bugling and staying put. Don't be afraid to really push him. Work the cover and wind effectively, and get as close as you dare. Run—breaking branches, bugling, and thrashing trees as you go. Approach within 50 yards of the bull if you can, and go no farther. You'll never be able to precisely pinpoint his location, and he'll likely move around as well.

SITUATION #5

DATE: October 20
WEATHER: cool in the day—highs in the 40's, dropping below freezing in the evening.
VEGETATION: aspens throughout in the mid-elevations up to 7,500 feet, spruce and fir in higher elevations.
TOPOGRAPHY: rolling country with some extensive heavily timbered plateaus.
HUNTING PRESSURE: moderate to heavy.
ROAD ACCESS: extensive.
GENERAL DESCRIPTION: Here's the classic opening day situation. The general hunt begins, with hunters everywhere. The rut is over; bugling is nonexistent. With so much competition from other hunters, you must try something unique, or be extremely lucky.

OPTION #1: If you'll take the first legal elk that comes along, consider using other hunters to drive elk to you. Early on opening morning, well before shooting light, position yourself on a high vantage point, preferably in a saddle or high on a slope where you have good visibility below. Stay there as long as you can—all day if possible. Hunters moving about are apt to spook elk and push them around.

OPTION #2: Get out your map or rely on your knowledge of the country. As I've said many times in this book, hunt areas least disturbed by other hunters. Few people will climb steep slopes. Often you'll find elk in such places, and in the worst tangles of timber imaginable. The farther away from roads you get, the better. Use the cow call when you walk through the timber. Pay attention to every noise you hear. A pop of a twig could mean the silent approach of another elk. Be aware of every sound in the woods. Use the call most extensively when elk are moving from feeding to bedding areas and vice-versa early in the morning and late in the afternoon.

SITUATION #6

DATE: November 10
WEATHER: cold—highs in mid-20's, dropping to around zero at night. Snow is present, from four to six inches in mid-elevations to two or three feet in higher elevations.
VEGETATION: pine and spruce, with large open sagebrush expanses.

Hunting Strategies That Work 143

Knowledge of elk habits in your area are important. Zumbo shot this bull at a waterhole when the elk came over for a drink.

TOPOGRAPHY: steep to gentle slopes, flat areas on benches and lower elevations.
HUNTING PRESSURE: moderate.
ROAD ACCESS: most roads closed by Forest Service; access is via major road systems.
GENERAL DESCRIPTION: Because of heavy snow in the high country, you're convinced the migration has started. Few hunters are about, most of them glassing from vehicles for moving elk.
   OPTION #1: Most elk will be traveling through the timber, and may move a short distance each day. Elk that normally live in lower elevations might not have started to move, because of the comparatively lighter snow cover. Prepare to walk several miles a day, cutting for tracks. If you're in good elk country, you should come across fresh tracks sooner or later. When you do, try to identify a bull's track (if you're after a bull) by the much larger track. Follow as long as you can, being quiet as possible. If the woods are

noisy, blow a cow call every now and then. Have essential survival gear in your daypack, and prepare to hunt right up to dark. Elk will normally begin feeding before dark because they'll be hungry in the cold weather and have to work harder and longer to find food under the snow. The key to this option is to walk, walk, and walk some more, and get out there as early as possible and to stay out as late as you can. This is a prime time to glass—and I mean *really* glass. Elk are more easily spotted in snow, and they'll be feeding longer in the morning to find adequate food under the snow covering.

Chapter 19

Get It Out of the Woods

As I've said repeatedly in this book, the toughest part of elk hunting is getting it from where it fell to a road. The easiest way is to hire someone to do it, such as hiring an outfitter or packer, or, if you're hunting on your own, to shoot the animal next to a road or at least where you can drive to it. But let's say that the animal falls some distance from a road. That's when the old saying, "the fun of the hunt is over when you squeeze the trigger," becomes so very true. That's assuming, of course, that you hit what you're aiming at.

The obvious necessity of transporting your prize out of the forest may be an arduous task, perhaps requiring more energy and muscle than you possess. That's the major difference between big game hunting and other forms of hunting. Carrying out a bunch of pheasants or ducks is a no-brainer.

The task is much more complicated if you walk up to your downed 700 pound bull elk on the backside of Forgotten Ridge, or your 450 pound cow elk that unfortunately fell at the bottom of Lonesome Valley, with no road close by. In either situation, you're faced with an urgent chore, especially if it's warm and you must cool the carcass as quickly as possible.

It would be splendid if we could drive to every carcass, or at least be accompanied by a bunch of husky pals who would make short work of retrieving the animal. Since that's not always the case, we must be prepared for any eventuality.

Packing an elk's head can be a big job. Here, outfitter Frank Simms carries out a bull taken by General Chuck Yeager.

TAG IT FIRST

Your first act upon reaching your prize and admiring it is to tag it and make everything nice and legal. Most states require you to tag your animal immediately upon approaching it, or before you transport it out of the woods. Some regulations allow you to keep the tag in your pocket until you reach camp or your vehicle, as long as the tag is initially filled out at the kill site. Be sure you know the precise rules, since game wardens are not sympathetic to your pleas of ignorance of the law. The rules are clearly spelled out in the free pamphlet supplied by the state wildlife agency. Improper tagging of big game is one of the most common big game hunting violations. There's no need to get a ticket because you weren't aware of the law.

FIELDDRESSING

The very next task after punching out your tag is to eviscerate the animal, and this must be done immediately. If you want to take pictures first, do so in speedy fashion. Internal organs and liquids must be quickly removed from the carcass, otherwise the meat will spoil because of bacterial action and contact with blood and other materials interrupted by the bullet. A rule of thumb is to fielddress

the animal no later than one hour after it's expired. If you hit the elk and it ran off, taking some time to find it, start fielddressing *immediately*. If the carcass has started to bloat, it can still be salvaged, but you must work fast. If the temperature is very cold, an hour's delay in fielddressing might be acceptable, but no longer.

Some people advise cutting the animal's throat to "bleed it" after it's dead by cutting the jugular vein with a knife. Don't bother. Once the animal's heart stops, little or no blood will issue from any vein or artery. Bleeding is therefore a waste of time, and the unnecessary neck cut might cause problems with a taxidermist if you want to mount the head.

Dressing the animal is a simple matter of slitting the body cavity from the anus to the chest, taking care not to puncture internal organs. With the initial slit made, you merely reach in, cut away connective tissues, and pull the organs out of the cavity. It's far easier to remove the entrails by cutting through the brisket and ribs as close to the throat as you can. Believe me, it's a very long reach in to the cavity with your arms if you must stop at the brisket. The only reason you'd do that is to avoid the extra labor in sawing through the ribs, or to avoid the cut altogether if the animal is being caped. Saw through those rib bones if you can. It will make dressing far easier.

The best way to learn the process is to accompany an experienced hunter and observe. If you're the rare individual who intends to try this by yourself for the first time, it's best to rent one of the many videos on the subject and watch it closely. Looking at illustrations or photos in a book is largely a waste of time, since almost no one carries a book in the field, and even if you did, the photos or drawings are poor guidelines when you're standing over the carcass with a sharp knife.

If your elk fell in a nasty spot, you may have to do a great deal of difficult maneuvering and positioning to get to the underside of the carcass. An ordeal may be awaiting if your prize has fallen in an awkward position on a steep slope, or in very heavy brush or timber. I recall a solo hunt in which I spent two hours to simply roll a bull elk over onto its back so I could begin the fielddressing process.

It's a good idea to carry 50 feet of lightweight rope in your daypack to hold the carcass securely from sliding down a steep hillside as you work on it, or to tie off the legs away from your work area.

COOL AND PROTECT IT

Be acutely aware that the carcass be cooled as soon as possible. Once the fielddressing is done, move the carcass or quarters into the shade if you must leave it and return with some help. If you can't move the carcass, protect it from the sun by loosely piling branches on top. Leave plenty of room for air to circulate. In the event the weather is warm, make every effort to get the carcass to a locker plant where it can be aged in a cooler. Your elk is a priority. Forget about everything else, from helping out on drives with your buddies, to camp chores, or whatever. Again, I repeat. Get it cool quickly.

Various animals, birds, insects, and perhaps unscrupulous humans may want to share your good fortune as well. If you leave the carcass unattended, protect it from unwanted pests. Birds and human thieves can be thwarted by literally hiding a carcass under a pile of branches, sticks, and whatever forest debris is available. Use loose evergreen boughs, and be sure to cover areas where there have been incisions made, since ravens, jays, and magpies will try their best to find a way to the feast.

With a lot of help, you might try to move a big bull by dragging it.

You shouldn't have much problem with people stealing your game in a remote area or on private land, but you should be wary if you're hunting public land crowded with plenty of hunters. If you have a camera, take a series of close-ups of your animal if it's a bull. In the event someone steals your animal and challenges you to prove it, your photos will hold up in court or before a game warden. Another precaution is to hide a coin somewhere in the animal's cavity by making a slit in the flesh and sliding the coin in. When confronting a thief who has your animal, go with a game warden and produce the coin from the spot you hid it.

Never make a bold challenge to someone you believe has stolen your animal if you're alone. Always be accompanied by a law enforcement officer. It's a sad commentary on the hunting fraternity that we should concern ourselves with thievery, but that's unfortunately an all-too common human trait that exists in every segment of society.

Coyotes, bears, and other mammals may move in on a carcass left overnight. Because of its natural wariness, a coyote may wait a day or two for human scent to dissipate before moving in on a carcass, so it's unlikely they'll cause you much grief. A bear, on the other hand, will begin devouring your prize as soon as it discovers it, but it may take a bear a couple of days to catch a whiff of the carcass. By that time you should have the meat out of the woods.

If you're hunting an area that has plentiful fresh bear sign and you must leave the carcass overnight, try to hang the meat at least seven or eight feet off the ground. Do this by tying a rope to the meat, throwing the rope over a stout branch, and pulling the meat up to the desired height. Of course, you'll have to quarter the carcass in order to handle it.

I recall an elk hunt with my daughter Judi when a bear moved in on her fine six point bull during the evening. Judi killed the bull very late in the afternoon, and we were a long way from camp, so we had no choice but to leave the carcass. Luckily, the bear hadn't discovered the elk until early the next morning and hadn't done much damage prior to our return. Had the bear come upon the carcass sooner, it could easily have made off with a good portion of our quality meat.

You might discourage predators from approaching the carcass by tying some clothes on and around the meat. Sometimes your scent will discourage animals from getting too close.

Trying to keep insects away can be a monumental problem if you're hunting in very warm weather. There exists, unfortunately, a pest known as a blowfly, which is simply a larger version of our common housefly. Blowflies show up almost instantly after the prize hits the ground, and their numbers will increase into the hundreds during fielddressing when more odors from the carcass are released into the atmosphere.

You cannot keep the determined flies away, unless a companion sits closely and constantly flails at the buzzing insects as they attempt to land. That's the way it's done in Africa, but there you have the luxury of having several idle helpers around, all of them quite willing to flog away at flies. To protect the carcass from blowflies and still allow air to circulate and cool the meat after fielddressing is accomplished, wrap the animal with plenty of cheesecloth. Use several layers, since flies can sometimes penetrate the webbing of a single cheesecloth layer.

Despite your precautions, flies may lay eggs on the meat. These show up as small white bundles containing hundreds of eggs. When you spot them, simply scrape them off. If they go undiscovered, they will hatch in 24 hours or so, transformed into tiny maggots which grow rapidly. Maggot-infested meat should be immediately cut away and discarded.

SKINNING

The need to skin an animal in the woods or at camp depends on several factors, notably the air temperature, and mode of transporting the animal out of the woods. If you intend on dragging quarters, or have enough help to drag the whole elk, leave the skin intact to protect the meat as the carcass is being dragged. This is standard practice, unless you're hunting in extremely hot weather and want to skin the animal quickly to help cool the meat. During some early seasons, especially August and September bowhunts, the air temperature commonly hits eighty degrees or more. In that event, you want to skin the carcass as soon as possible.

An animal can be skinned where it lays in the forest, or in a more convenient place where it can be hung and then worked on. The latter is by far the easiest method, but isn't always possible, unless you have a winch or can get a rope over a branch and use a vehicle to lift the carcass off the ground.

Skinning tools are simple, amounting to a sharp knife and a sharpening stone. Ideally, a skinning knife should have a curved blade, because you're cutting parallel with the surface of the flesh rather than making a crosscut incision. A sharp-pointed long knife is apt to puncture the hide.

If you must skin an elk that lies on the ground, take precautions to keep the meat clean. I carry a lightweight space blanket in my daypack that I roll the skinned carcass on when I'm finished with the upper side. The blanket keeps the flesh from making contact with the ground. If the meat touches the ground, it will invariably pick up plenty of unwanted dirt, twigs, pine needles, and other particles.

Skinning an elk where it falls may be a several-hour job, especially if it's lying in brush or a hard to reach area.

Another option is to carefully roll the carcass onto the loose hide you've skinned as you begin working on the opposite flank. Either way, you'll be glad you made the extra effort to keep the meat clean when you get it home or to a processing plant.

If the weather turns bitterly cold, try not to let the carcass freeze rock hard if you intend on cutting it up yourself. You may have a heck of a time thawing it.

AGING

For quality meat, you should allow the carcass to age for a week or more at 35°F to 40°F or so. Be sure the meat is hanging at least five feet off the ground if dogs are running loose, since canines are quite fond of fresh venison. I recall an incident when a neighbor's dog helped herself to the hindquarters of a nice buck that was hanging from a beam inside my garage. I had the door propped open about eighteen inches to let air circulate. Unfortunately, the opening was just high enough to admit the dog. That particular buck deer had cost me and my pals a great deal of sweat to remove from the woods, so I was mighty unhappy to discover that the dog had enjoyed about five pounds of quality rump steaks.

The author was able to get this cow to a place where he could hang the carcass and saw it in quarters.

BONING

By boning a carcass, you leave much unwanted weight in the field. When you eliminate the bones, you decrease the weight by ten to twenty five percent or more. Boning is environmentally friendly, too. Bones left in the woods will decay and return to the earth, or feed rodents who in turn indirectly transfer bones to the soil.

Boning is a simple task, requiring some cheesecloth, a packsack or rucksack, a knife with a long, flexible blade, and a knife sharpener. A fish fillet knife makes an excellent boning tool; I've used the same one for years. My favorite is a Buck fillet knife with a blade that nicely folds into the handle.

The actual process of boning doesn't require you to have advanced education in meat-cutting or butchering. Simply learn as you go, carving out large chunks of meat. As soon as you free a piece, wrap it in clean cheesecloth and lay it in the shade where it will cool quickly. Complete the job in one operation, and hang the surplus meat that you can't carry from tree branches, allowing the breeze to circulate through the cheesecloth.

QUARTERING

An elk is almost always quartered to bring it out of the woods. Some hunters and outfitters may prefer to split a carcass in half lengthwise, but quartering is most common. To quarter an animal, you'll need a very sharp meat saw, and enough countenance to persist until the job is done. Meat saws come in a variety of shapes and models, and all hunting saws are portable and compact to the point where they can be carried on a belt holster.

There's an alternative to quartering a carcass with a saw. Simply slice off each of the legs at the joints. Then cut away all flank, rib, and neck meat, the backstraps, and cut through the ribs to reach in and remove the tenderloins. No sawing is required, and you'll get every ounce of meat that you would have removed if you took the quarters out whole.

Doing this is a modified boning operation. You've eliminated the need to saw through tough bones, and you still have four quarters, but they're obviously much smaller and lighter. The meat you bone away from the carcass will need to be kept clean and thoroughly cooled. Use cheesecloth as you normally would if you were boning it all.

DRAGGING

To drag an elk, grab hold of an antler and pull it to your destination. This is only possible if you have plenty of husky pals and the route out is downhill, the steeper the better. Otherwise, dragging may be out of the question. If it's a female, you can grab an ear or tie a rope around the neck and start dragging. Make no mistake; this is tough, tough work.

When you drag the entire carcass or piece of it, make the job easier by first determining a route. Plan the course so you can avoid downed logs, patches of brush, and subtle little inclines that will become immediately noticeable when you drag. It's a great deal easier to drag with your shoulders than pull with your hands. Some commercially made harnesses are available, or you can make your own with a rope or strap, which is wrapped around your upper torso and under your arms.

A carcass drags easier if you can lift the head and shoulders off the ground. Less friction means less resistance. Tie the front legs up around the neck of the animal so they don't catch in brush as you pull, or cut them off completely at the knee joint.

A number of products are sold that help you drag, such as a sled or piece of heavy-duty plastic that will slide easier over the ground.

CARRY IT OUT

Backpacking requires you to haul the meat out on your shoulders. You can do this in two ways—either carry a quarter, or carry boned meat.

A quarter is best carried by lashing it to a packframe. Many models and designs are on the market today. A quarter of an elk may weigh from 80 to 100 pounds, which is a big load, especially when considering the nasty terrain. Use good judgment when you plan on packing a quarter out, and remember, you'll have four quarters to contend with, plus the head and cape if you're bringing them out. If your animal is a mile or two from a road, it could take a couple days to get it moved. Most meat quarters are carried by horses, but some hunters in reasonably good physical condition attempt it themselves.

Boned meat is best carried in a rucksack or a packbasket similar to what trappers use to carry their gear. Always wrap boned meat in cheesecloth to protect it from dirt and insects.

WHEEL IT OUT

It's often said that the invention of the wheel changed the course of civilization. That's true, especially from the hunter's perspective. If you're handy with tools, you can manufacture a carrier that will accommodate 150 to 200 pounds. Be sure to equip it with brakes so you can stop forward motion when going downhill.

Several models are commercially made and can be purchased from mail order catalogs or sporting goods stores.

I use a commercial model frequently, and have wheeled elk, deer, and moose out of remote areas. Without the carrier, I would have expended a great deal more muscle, energy, sweat, and tears in getting the meat out.

This is the end result—superb, natural healthy meat that contains the "good" cholesterol, little fat, and no steroids, antibiotics, nor additives given to livestock.

USE A POLE CARRY

By lashing a quarter or two to the middle of a stout pole and having a hunter carry each end, you'll reduce the load considerably. I've moved 200 pounds of elk meat several miles by coordinating a pole carry with a buddy.

Some tips—be sure to use a stout pole that won't break under the weight of the carcass. It should be as lightweight as possible to save undue wear and tear on your shoulders. Lash the quarter(s) securely so it doesn't swing from side to side as it's being carried. The swinging motion will make it difficult to keep your balance. Pad your carrying shoulder with an extra shirt, jacket, heavy glove—whatever you have to cushion the weight of the load.

For safety's sake, even though a hunter clad in orange is at each end of the pole, drape the meat generously with orange flagging to identify it as something already dead, especially if there's any fur attached to the quarters.

USE A HORSE

Moving meat with a horse is tricky business. Don't attempt it unless you have experience around horses *and* know how to pack. Some hunters rent pack horses after they've taken game and transport the meat out to a road. This is also risky business, because some horses for hire have never packed game. That being the case, you may be involved in a little rodeo, and someone—either the horse or a hunter, can get badly hurt. Before renting a horse, know its packing history. Practically every horse must be broken to pack wild meat.

Know your pack equipment and knots, because you'll use that information extensively. Panniers, which are a pair of containers made out of wood, canvas, plastic, or metal, are most commonly used to pack gear and meat. A sturdy horse will carry up to 200 pounds of dead weight, but less is better, and the load must be almost perfectly balanced as well, weighing almost the same on each side.

GET IT HOME

Many hunters who travel long distances from home prefer to have their big game processed locally, and then have it shipped home by the processor. Another option, if the hunter is flying, is to take the processed meat along on the same flight by checking it in as baggage.

If you intend to use a processor's services, make arrangements in advance, or at least inquire about their scheduling. Of course, when you make advance inquiry, you don't know if you'll successfully bring in an animal, but it's a good idea to know the meat company's policy. In some busy western towns, you'll need to bring your meat in two or three days before your departure date if you want to take it with you. If you hunt with an outfitter, he'll often provide that service for you, but be sure it's included in his price. Some outfitters charge extra for meat handling once you return from hunting camp.

Many processors, especially in the west, will make a variety of salami, baloney, and sausages from your meat. Be aware that it's illegal to buy wild game in all fifty states, but you will be charged a processing fee depending on the kind of meat you request. In some cases, you can trade your meat for an equal amount of already processed game, but you'll still be charged the processing fee.

If you're hunting close to home, you can simply stow the animal's carcass in your vehicle's trunk or in the back of your pickup. Given public attitudes on hunting these days, it's a good idea to transport your meat so it's not visible. Having the dead animal exposed is distasteful to many people. Ethics suggest that we consider the sensitivities of others.

In the event you're traveling a long distance with an overnight stop or two, take precautions to keep the meat cool and clean. Obviously, if the outside temperature is cool, you can transport the meat with no special considerations.

Many hunters use a homemade insulated box to transport frozen or chilled meat. To keep frozen meat hard, put a quantity of dry ice on it. To keep it chilled, if the weather is warm and you have no meat box, tightly wrap the already chilled meat in an old quilt or sleeping bag. It will keep for up to two or three days.

For great recipes, try the author's cookbook. Order it for $16.95 plus shipping and handling by calling 1-800-673-4868, or see the web site: www.jimzumbo.com.

If you're shipping more than one elk, consider renting a trailer to accommodate the meat. Rent the trailer as soon as possible, especially if you're renting in a small, popular hunting town, since most units will already be rented.

There's no mystery in flying meat, either frozen or chilled. To fly it frozen, put dry ice with it (the quantity depends on the amount of meat and size of container—ask a local processor for advice) and be sure you tell the airline clerk you're shipping dry ice, since the ice is governed by FAA regulations. To ship chilled meat, wrap it in cheesecloth or butcher paper, and then wrap it with several layers of newspaper. Place it in at least two garbage bags to avoid leakage, and put the garbage bags in a duffel bag or suitcase; or pack it in a cooler. Be sure the total weight of each container does not exceed 70 pounds, since that's the standard maximum airline limit.

Most airlines will allow you to ship three baggage items; anything more will be charged a modest fee. It's far cheaper to ship your meat on the same plane as you travel than by sending it air freight. Another plus is that the meat will be with you when you arrive at your home destination.

You can send your meat air freight by having a processor handle the arrangements. Another option is to send it via one of the next-day services such as Federal Express, UPS next-day air, or one of the others. Be forewarned that this is extremely expensive. Shipping by rail or bus isn't a good idea because of the time it takes.

However you ship your meat, think *cool*. Refrigeration is absolutely critical for your prize to arrive home in an edible condition.

CHAPTER 20

THE GOOD OLD DAYS ARE RIGHT NOW

It was during the summer of 1962 when I'd seen the elk track. Having never seen one before, I hurriedly reported the find to my wildlife professor. My class had been doing field work during a wildlife course at Utah State University, with most of our studies directed toward mule deer. Elk were scarce in the forest, and up to that point, none of us students had seen one.

The professor examined the track, confirmed that it indeed was an elk, and allowed as to how fortunate we were to have seen it. Though we worked in the forest the rest of the summer, we never laid eyes on a living, breathing elk.

The old professor is gone now, but the elk aren't. In fact, they're present in such numbers that they're using up the range almost as fast as it can grow.

That's the case throughout most of the west. As hunters, we're familiar with wildlife success stories in terms of the enormous increases in animals today compared to their numbers at the turn of the century. Whitetails have made unbelievable gains, and so have muleys, antelope, turkeys and other species. But elk have an intriguing story, quite different from other game.

When America was settled, elk ranged from the east to west coast. Six subspecies lived in our country, roaming in eastern hardwood forests, the central plains, and in the western mountains. A common notion prevails that elk were plains animals and were driven into the mountains by settlers and market hunters.

Biologists refute that theory, pointing to scientific data suggesting that elk are newcomers to America, having come here about 10,000 years ago from Siberia during the Ice Age. They were animals of both the mountains and the plains, with estimates of 10 million elk inhabiting North America. The reason remnant elk populations were able to hold on in the mountains is simple: they were harder to hunt, thus the easier plains elk quickly disappeared.

It didn't take very long for elk to be driven to extinction in many areas. The Eastern elk disappeared before the turn of the 19th century; the Merriams around 1904. Other subspecies also dwindled rapidly. Around 1920, the major species, which is the Rocky Mountain elk, numbered fewer than 50,000 animals, most of them in Yellowstone Park and the National Elk Refuge in Wyoming. Other than their superb tasting flesh and the fact that they competed with livestock for range grass, their tusks or ivories also contributed to their downfall. Bulls and cows alike have a pair of unique teeth that are highly esteemed as jewelry. Historical accounts state that untold numbers of elk were killed exclusively for their teeth. By 1910, it appeared that elk were headed for extinction.

Then began the unique aspect of the elk success story. From those two Wyoming locations, between 1892 to 1939, about 5,200 elk were transplanted to 36 states and Canada via rail, wagon, and trucks. An all-out effort was made involving thousands of people to put elk back in America. The result? Today, according to the Rocky Mountain Elk Foundation, there are approximately 960,000 elk in the U.S. and Canada. The one million mark is just around the corner. A map of the transplant efforts resembles a huge wheel, with spokes emanating from the Wyoming hub.

Why have elk made such dramatic increases? A combination of factors created population booms. Forest fires and logging encouraged elk by producing the kind of forage preferred by the animals. More restrictive seasons and hunts protected female elk, encouraging herd expansion. Increased transplant programs, continuing to this day, allow elk to establish themselves in historic habitats where they are currently absent but once flourished.

This enormous success story has not come about painlessly. In the viewpoint of some cattlemen (but *not* all), every bite of grass

taken by an elk is one less bite for a cow. Efforts by state agencies to introduce elk were commonly opposed not only by ranchers, but by the U.S. Forest Service and U.S. Bureau of Land Management, two federal agencies that control almost half a billion acres in America.

The author's good hunting pal, Jack Atcheson, Sr., with a dandy bull he took 30 years ago. Thanks to good management, Jack and other modern hunters are still taking good bulls.

What did the feds have against elk? As guardians of public lands, both agencies are mandated to manage lands under a multiple use system. Unfortunately, multiple use seldom favors all uses, but ranks them in order of priority. Until recently, livestock grazing was a far higher priority than wildlife management. I recall attending many so-called "interagency" meetings in Utah when I worked as a wildlife biologist. The Forest Service consistently gave in to rancher's demands and allowed cow elk hunting on ranges that had the potential of supporting many more elk. As a result, elk herds were maintained at low levels. On some Utah national forests, federal officials were so closely aligned with cattlemen that forest rangers wouldn't allow elk to be transplanted into their districts because it was all "allotted" to cattle. For many years there were zero elk in those forests, but happily, those days are over.

According to Mike Welch, big game coordinator for the Utah Division of Wildlife Resources, elk are flourishing in that state. "We have about 60,000 elk in Utah," Welch says. "They occupy practically all of their historic habitat, and are at their highest levels since being reintroduced from Wyoming about 80 years ago."

As a longtime resident of Utah, I watched those herds grow enormously, from the day I spotted that strange track as a college student in the early 60's. In 1970, 14,000 lived in Utah. In just over 25 years, 46,000 more elk joined their ranks. So many more elk, in fact, that recently the state allowed hunters to take two elk, one of which had to be antlerless. Also recently, Wyoming allowed an extra antlerless elk to be taken. These are unprecedented hunts. Never in modern history has a state allowed more than one elk to be killed. Obviously, elk are doing too well in some areas, and efforts are being taken to trim their numbers.

More big news for elk hunters comes from Colorado, the number one elk hunting state in terms of elk numbers, hunter harvest, and numbers of elk hunters. In 1998, hunters were allowed to purchase, across the counter, either-sex elk licenses for the general season in 48 units.

The highest harvest record in any state was Colorado's whopping 51,595 elk taken in l990. No other state has come even close to that figure.

Arizona and New Mexico also show amazing statistics regarding their elk herds and harvests. In 1975, Arizona hunters took about 1,100 elk; in 1995, more than 10,000 were killed. New Mexico hunters shot 1,800 elk in 1975, and more than 12,000 in l995. Nevada had zero elk in 1975, and now has a growing herd of more than 3,500 animals. California's Tule elk have grown in numbers from 600 in 1975 to more than 3,000. Despite animal rights protests, Tule elk hunts have been held in California for the last half dozen years.

Of the western elk states, only Washington shows declining elk harvests. This is the smallest state in the West, but it has the second highest human population, next to California. There seems to be little hope for Washington, with enormous growth predicted for years to come. Too many people and rapidly dwindling habitat seems to be taking its toll. According to wildlife officers, more than 30,000 acres each year are being lost to development and human encroachment.

Elk are doing fabulously well in other states outside the west. Herds are increasing dramatically, and in some states, brand new herds have been recently established. Arkansas is one of the hot success stories. With no elk in 1975, the population has climbed to almost 500. Arkansas had its first elk hunt ever in 1998. South Dakota's elk are in great shape, increasing from none in 1975 to almost 4,000. In 1995, 25 elk were introduced into Wisconsin. Those elk are doing remarkably well, and are expected to expand their numbers appreciably. Many other states are reporting expanding elk herds. Canada's elk herds have grown rapidly, increasing from 40,000 in 1975 to 89,000 in 1995.

Ed Rozman with the most legendary elk of all—the long-standing world record taken by John Plute in the late 1800s. A bigger elk was officially accepted by the Boone and Crockett Club in 1998.

With this wonderful success story, you'd think that elk hunting would be easier than ever. That's wishful thinking. Averaging hunter success in all the western states, elk hunters continue to have only a 20 to 25 percent hunter success rate.

There's a mighty logical reason for that. Though there are more elk, they continue to live in the most rugged landscape in the lower 48. The mountains remain as steep as ever, and the forests are still there—presenting the same formidable obstacles. Elk hunting will always be a physical challenge in much of the West.

Less than 50,000 elk lived in North America in the early part of this century. Now, more than 900,000 inhabit the country, and it's predicted there will be a million elk soon.

Hunting strategies themselves have radically changed over the last few decades. I remember making my own homemade bugle calls out of a chunk of garden hose, a length of pipe, or a willow branch. Granted, the sound that emanated from these instruments was tinny and quite unlike the bugle of a live elk, but they nonetheless worked. Then came along the diaphragm call which added an amazing new dimension to elk hunting. In reality, the call was first used for turkey hunting, and it's most commonly believed that call-maker Wayne Carlton was first to modify the sound and imitate an elk. Dozens of diaphragm models are on the market these days, used with or without a grunt tube. A big drawback is the difficulty in learning to use them. Since they fit entirely in your mouth, they often cause a gag reflex.

The next big discovery to hit the hunt scene was when Montana hunter Don Laubach realized that imitating a cow elk's chirp could have a profound implication in hunting strategies. Laubach gave me one of his prototype calls in the early 1980s and asked me to experiment with it. I did, was immediately impressed with the results, and wrote the first story ever on cow calling. Titled: "Elk Hunting's Newest Secret," it appeared in a 1986 issue of OUTDOOR LIFE. Soon afterward, Laubach's name became a household word among elk hunters, and his unique call became the hottest ticket in elk hunting gadgetry. Now, cow calling is routine, and more than a dozen manufacturers make the calls.

Not everyone is happy with the elk success story; the big animals cause serious damage to the ranching and farming industry. In places where elk are overpopulated, starvation may occur when forage is depleted. Game departments minimize these impacts by issuing antlerless tags to keep elk in check with the carrying capacity of the range.

I'm one of the many happy hunters who have no problem with taking a cow elk here and there. I'm also more than pleased if I'm fortunate enough to tie my tag to a bull. As the old saying goes, any elk is a good elk. And you might say that the good old days are *not* gone forever. When it comes to elk hunting, they're here right now. And now's also the time to get an easy elk. It's never been better.

Dan Zumbo, author's son, carries on his dad's tradition. Hunting, like other traditions, must be passed from one generation to another.

CHAPTER 21

THE FUTURE OF HUNTING

Every hunter is aware of the threats to the sport. A growing legion of anti-hunters is bound and determined to completely eliminate sport hunting in America. They wage all sorts of smear campaigns to discredit hunters, blaming us for a variety of problems. They exaggerate the truth and tell outright lies. To them, a hunter is a barbaric murderer who has no soul or conscience.

Sadly, it's virtually impossible to discuss hunting intelligently with these individuals. They are immune to logic and scientific conclusions, preferring instead to turn a deaf ear and continue their anti-hunting crusade.

Animal rights groups have made headway in their promises to end hunting, and are gearing up for all the victories they can win. Cougar hunting in California, for example, was banned forever by a public referendum in the ballot box. This was done despite the fact that there are more cougars in California than any other state, and the big cats are overpopulating to the point where they're attacking people. Colorado voters also agreed to terminate for all time spring bear hunting and baiting. Bear populations in Colorado have never been in jeopardy. Grizzly bear hunting was halted in Montana, thanks to animal rights groups who took their case to a federal judge. Only problem grizzlies were hunted prior to the ban—bears that were persistently destructive and dangerous.

Angela Zumbo, the author's youngest daughter, is pleased with her muley buck. She's proud of her deer, and enjoys hunting as much as anyone.

None of these issues are biologically founded, but are based on emotions, ignorance, and misinformation.

Despite this bleak appraisal, the picture is not all that gloomy. Eighty percent of Americans are non-hunters who have no strong opinions either way about the sport; 10 percent are activist anti-hunters, and 10 percent are hunters. Hunting has strong supporters in all levels of politics, and many prominent sportsmen continue to use their influence to promote hunting.

The future is with our youngsters. Zumbo is all smiles as he poses with his daughter, Janette, and her first buck.

Because hunters contribute millions of dollars annually for conservation, their financial support funds many wildlife management programs. When hunter's fees are used to protect habitat, game birds and animals aren't the only benefactors. Hundreds of other non-game species also benefit, including a large variety of song birds, small mammals, hawks, eagles, owls, endangered species and other creatures.

Hunters also pump hundreds of millions of dollars annually into local economies, particularly in small towns that depend on

those revenues each fall.

The bottom line is that hunters are welcomed by a broad segment of society, and it's unlikely that those attitudes will change dramatically in the near future.

Elk habitat is being reduced drastically each year because of a variety of factors. Fortunately, mining companies now reclaim areas, restoring them as they once were. Human encroachment is one of the biggest problems.

One of the biggest threats to hunting is rapid urbanization of rural areas. Farmlands make way for housing developments, shopping malls, summer homes, and other so-called "progressive" changes. Consequently, hunting areas continue to disappear as land is developed. Practically every middle-aged hunter can look back to where he was raised and recount sad tales about boyhood hunting spots being converted into paved parking lots. With this loss of hunting land comes a growing disinterest of hunting because it's simply too difficult to find a place to hunt. Many landowners these days post their lands and either prohibit hunting altogether, reserve it for family and friends, or lease it to hunting groups and outfitters. Many leases are high-priced, unaffordable by many hunters.

Another serious threat to hunting is the gradual decline in interest among youngsters. No activity can persist without constant recruitment. If the hunting tradition is to be continued, it must be passed on from one generation to another.

Children raised in cities often have no interest in the outdoors, and youngsters from single-parent families often have no opportunity to hunt because they lack a mentor. Many organizations are currently involved in introducing children to outdoor activities, but the best solution is for parents to acquaint their children to hunting at early ages.

A basic fundamental about hunting conveniently overlooked by anti-hunters is the fact that no species is hunted unless it produces a surplus that can be removed by hunting. Wildlife managers set seasons and bag limits to insure that the species is self-perpetuating.

Contrary to ridiculous claims made by animal rights groups, no endangered species has been hunted in modern times, nor has modern hunting ever contributed to a species being placed on the endangered species list.

Ironically enough, people who clamor the loudest for animal rights work toward only one objective—to allow all animals to live "natural" lives and not be pursued by hunters. What they fail to understand is the basic fact that man is part of the natural world and has been a major predator for thousands of years.

Thanks to transplant programs like this, elk are being moved into places they haven't inhabited for decades.

It's perfectly fine, according to anti-hunters, for an animal to die of natural causes. If those people could witness animals that die naturally, they might change their attitudes. It's often an agonizing, painful death. No veterinarian is present to humanely put a wild animal to sleep. In areas where hunting isn't allowed, animal populations commonly increase to the point where starvation or disease wipes out a large part of the population.

Hunters need to be vigilant to threats from anti-hunters and defend the sport at every level by joining organizations that lobby for hunting rights. Hunters must also follow the rules of ethics, conducting themselves accordingly, both in public and in the woods.

As far as the future of elk goes, it couldn't be brighter. Soon, more than one million elk will roam North America, thanks to concerned citizens, state wildlife agencies, and the Rocky Mountain Elk Foundation. Without question, we are enjoying the best of elk hunting since this country was settled.

APPENDIX

Where to Find Your Easy Elk

Any time you try to pinpoint outstanding hunting spots, you get in trouble. The best hunting is in places where there is the lightest pressure, so by spotlighting those places, more people go there, thus the hunting worsens. I wish I could wave a magic wand and tell you exactly where to go in the state of your choice, but it doesn't work that way.

What I'll do here is to describe specific counties in each state that have the highest elk densities. I won't specifically name units, because elk populations fluctuate, and regulations are prone to change. I'll also list the phone numbers and addresses for each state wildlife management agency, the BLM state offices, as well as all the national forests. I'll specify those that have the highest elk populations. There will also be information on how to get statistical data from each state that tells you where and how to apply for limited entry areas.

Remember, this book is about how to get an easy elk—not just how to get a trophy elk. Big bulls almost always come from large private land holdings that are expensive to hunt, or public lottery-draw areas that are tough to draw. I'll mention a few of the latter, but note that these are popular units. Be aware that preference points and bonus points will help you get those lottery tags.

If you're serious about getting an elk the next time you go out, do some homework and check the state regulations for the top lottery draw areas. I'm sorry to repeat myself so many times, but the lottery draws are *the key* to an easy elk.

The following list includes 9 of the 11 western states that have significant elk populations. California and Nevada were not listed, but be aware that there are a few excellent lottery draw hunts in those states. Information is available from the respective state wildlife agencies: California Department of

Fish and Game, 1416 9th St., Sacramento, CA 95814; (916) 653-7664, and Nevada Department of Wildlife, Box 10678, Reno, NV 89520; (702) 688-1500.

ARIZONA

This arid southwest state is best known for its retirement attractions, but it's the top state for trophy elk. In 1985, when I wrote my book, HUNT ELK, I made this statement in the book: "Astute elk hunters know that Arizona has some of the biggest bulls in the West, and many are betting that the next world-record bull will come from this state." That prediction held true; the new world record was officially accepted into the B&C book in 1998.

About 50,000 elk live in Arizona, with about 10,000 harvested annually. Of that number, about one-third to one-half are antlerless. Despite its desert status, almost 7,000 square miles of elk country is in this state, the bulk of it along the Mogollon Rim from Flagstaff to the New Mexico border.

Arizona has the distinction of having the best tribal elk hunting in the country, with at least eight Indian reservations offering hunts. For general information, call the Bureau of Indian Affairs, (602) 379-4511.

The highest elk densities are in the southern half of Coconino County and the southern part of Apache County. There are also good numbers in Yavapai, Gila, and Navajo counties, as well as in the northern portions of Graham and Greenlee counties.

It would be impossible to pinpoint the top trophy areas because big bulls are scattered through the counties just mentioned. As a rule of thumb, draw a circle 50 miles around Flagstaff and you'll include some of the finest trophy bull country on the planet. If you can afford it, any of the Indian reservations offer superb hunting for giant bulls.

For good public land hunting in the areas of densest elk populations, best bets are the Coconino, Tonto, and Apache-Sitgreaves national forests.

All tags, both resident and nonresident, must be applied for in a lottery draw. Arizona offers bonus points; for information and statistics write the Arizona Game and Fish Department, 2221 W. Greenway Rd., Phoenix, AZ 85023; (602) 942-3000. A special publication called HUNT ARIZONA BOOK gives lottery statistics and is available for $5.00.

National Forest Directory for Arizona
Apache-Sitgreaves National Forest
 Federal Bldg., PO Box 640
 Springerville, AZ 85938
 (520) 333-4301
Coconino National Forest
 2323 E. Greenlaw Ln.
 Flagstaff, AZ 86004
 (602) 527-7400
Kaibab National Forest
 800 S. 6th St.
 Williams, AZ 86046
 (520) 635-8200
Prescott National Forest
 344 S. Cortez
 Prescott, AZ 86303
 (520) 771-4700
Tonto National Forest
 2324 E. McDowell Rd.
 Phoenix, AZ 85006
 (602) 225-5200
Bureau of Land Management State Office
 222 N. Central
 Phoenix, AZ 85004
 (602) 417-9200

COLORADO

This state contains almost one-fourth of the elk on the planet, with upwards of 200,000 to 220,000 roaming the western mountains. Colorado also has far more hunters than any other state, with about 200,000 pursuing elk each year. Because Colorado is the only major elk state that offers unlimited tags to residents and nonresidents alike, heavy hunting pressure is the rule. Hunters who fail to get tags in premier states such as Wyoming, Montana, and Idaho look to Colorado as a last resort. Typically anywhere from 40,000 to 50,000 elk are taken each year.

Because of heavy hunting pressure, few bulls survive long enough to grow large antlers, especially on public land or overhunted ranches. Consequently, raghorns and spikes are the most common.

Offsetting this dismal appraisal is an outstanding opportunity to take big bulls on many of the lottery draw units, and private holdings that offer a Ranching for Wildlife program. The latter is a concept where many large ranches offer tags to the public in return for more liberal hunting seasons. Both the public and private hunts are in the preference point system where you accumulate one point each year you apply until you've garnered enough to draw one of the precious tags. And precious they are: hunting success rates are very high for big bulls, and outfitters aren't required in many of the units.

My favorite spots to get a big, easy elk, are in Moffat County in the very northwest corner of the state. Most of the better units adjoin Dinosaur National Monument. Another top unit borders Estes National Park with special late tags geared to hunting elk migrating out of the park.

Colorado offers three separate seasons; you can choose only one. Many units protect spikes for one or more of the seasons, and some have a minimum number of points on

legal bulls. Cow tags are fairly easy to get in many of the units; beginning in 1998, either-sex tags were sold across the counter.

An early muzzleloader season is my choice for an easy firearms hunt without having to wait years to build preference points. Lately, one or two preference points are required to obtain a muzzleloader tag.

Colorado has plenty of public lands on national forests and BLM lands. Elk inhabit the mountains in the western half of the state, and are well represented in all the mountain ranges. However, the densities are highest in these counties if you're interested in an easy elk, but remember you'll have plenty of competition on public land: starting from the north, all of Routt and Eagle counties, the eastern portions of Rio Blanco, Garfield and Mesa counties, all of Delta and Gunnison counties, the eastern portion of Montrose County, and most of Dolores and LaPlata counties. In the south-central area, densest populations are in Costilla County, and the western half of Huerfano and Las Animas counties.

National forests containing the largest herds include the Routt, White River, Gunnison, Uncompahgre, San Juan, and San Isabel.

For information, contact the Colorado Division of Wildlife, 6060 Broadway, Denver, CO 80216; (303) 297-1192. For an excellent statistical breakdown of top units and preference point requirements, order the BIG-GAME STATS BOOK for $7.00.

NATIONAL FOREST DIRECTORY FOR COLORADO
Arapaho and Roosevelt National Forests
  240 W. Prospect
  Fort Collins, CO 80526
  (970) 498-1100

Grand Mesa, Uncompahgre, and Gunnison National Forests
2250 Highway 50
Delta, CO 81416
(970) 874-6600
Pike and San Isabel National Forests
1920 Valley Dr.
Pueblo, CO 81008
(719) 545-8737
San Juan-Rio Grande National Forests
1803 West Highway 160
Monte Vista, CO 81144
(719) 852-5941
White River National Forest
Old Federal Bldg.
9th and Grand
Box 948
Glenwood Springs, CO 81602
(970) 945-2521
Medicine Bow-Routt National Forests
(Medicine Bow is in Wyoming and Routt is in Colorado)
2468 Jackson St.
Laramie, WY 82070-6535
(307) 745-2300

Bureau of Land Management State Office
2850 Youngfield St.
Lakewood, CO 80215
(303) 239-3600

IDAHO

This is one of the premier elk states, with a booming population of almost 120,000 elk, placing Idaho second to Colorado in terms of elk numbers. During a typical year,

hunters take upwards of 25,000 animals.

Elk country in this state is like hunting two different worlds. The panhandle region is extremely thickly forested and damp, while the southern and central mountains are more like the rest of the Rockies.

Though elk are well scattered in the state, the highest densities are in the southern portion of Shoshone County, most of Clearwater County, and the north and south portions of sprawling Idaho County. Public lands are well represented here on the Clearwater and Nez Perce national forests.

Idaho's so-called "controlled hunts" offer lottery draws on many outstanding units. One of my favorite backcountry areas in all the west is the Selway Wilderness, chiefly along the Moose Creek drainage. There are some good hunts bordering Montana in the Island Park area, and don't overlook draw units near Boise. Be aware that some areas are spike-only. Cow tags are readily available, especially in the panhandle region. There are special early firearms hunts in some backcountry units during the September bugle season.

Resident tags are unlimited for general hunts, but there is a quota for nonresidents. These tags are sold on a first-come first-served basis. Part of the quota is reserved for outfitters.

For information, contact the Idaho Fish and Game Department, 600 S. Walnut, Box 25, Boise, ID 83707; (208) 334-3700. For information on drawing statistics on controlled hunts, request the free CONTROLLED-HUNT SUMMARY REPORT. No bonus or preference points are awarded in Idaho.

NATIONAL FOREST DIRECTORY FOR IDAHO
Clearwater National Forest
  12730 Highway 12
  Orofino, ID 83544
  (208) 476-4541

Idaho Panhandle National Forest
  3815 Schreiber Way
  Coeur d'Alene, ID 83815-8363
  (208) 765-7223
Nez Perce National Forest
  Rt. 2, Box 475
  Grangeville, ID 83530
  (208) 983-1950
Boise National Forest
  1249 S. Vinrell Way
  Boise, ID 83709
  (208) 373-4100
Caribou National Forest
  Federal Bldg., Suite 172
  250 S. 4th Ave.
  Pocatello, ID 83201
  (208) 236-7500
Challis and Salmon National Forests
  RR2, Box 600
  Salmon, ID 83467
  (208) 756-5100
Payette National Forest
  Box 1026
  800 W. Lakeside Ave.
  McCall, ID 83638
  (208) 634-0700
Sawtooth National Forest
  2647 Kimberly Rd. E.
  Twin Falls, ID 83301-7976
  (208) 737-3200
Targhee National Forest
  420 N. Bridge St.
  PO Box 208
  St. Anthony, ID 83445
  (208) 624-3151

Bureau of Land Management State Office
1387 S. Vinnell Way
Boise, ID 83709
(208) 373-4000

MONTANA

The biggest state in the Rockies has about 100,000 elk well distributed throughout the western region. Though most herds live in the steep mountains west of the Continental Divide, there are plenty of animals on smaller mountain ranges to the east.

The most northwesterly part of Montana has an abundance of precipitation and thick forests, while the rest of the elk habitat is characterized by less dense forests. Numerous wilderness areas offer remote hunting opportunities as well as early September firearms seasons.

If a hunter was invited to choose any unit in the state to hunt, he or she would invariably head for the late hunt at Gardiner. This is a premier spot since migrating elk cross out of Yellowstone and into the neighboring Gallatin National Forest. These hunts last four days for bulls and two days for cows, and run into early February. Huge bulls are taken here, many of them close to roads. While it's admittedly difficult to draw a bull tag, those who do often have the hunt of their life. Hunters after an easy cow have far better odds of drawing a late tag in Gardiner. Late bull hunts are also held for migrating animals along the Gallatin River between Big Sky and West Yellowstone.

Another outstanding hunt occurs on the sprawling C.M. Russell National Wildlife Refuge in the eastern region. Very big bulls inhabit this area, though firearms tags are tough to draw. Bowhunters find it much easier to obtain tags in this fabulous unit.

Ten national forests and plenty of BLM land offer exceptional public hunting, with substantial herds located on each forest. The Gallatin National Forest has some of the largest populations due to its proximity to Yellowstone National Park.

Montana has a very long five week elk season, starting in late October and running through Sunday of Thanksgiving Week. Many astute locals wait until the end of the season to hunt, counting on heavy snow in the high country driving elk to lowlands where they're more accessible.

Resident tags are unlimited, but nonresident tags are offered in a lottery. Currently, there are more nonresident applicants than there are tags available, but unsuccessful applicants receive a preference point and are guaranteed a tag the following year. This could change if more applicants try for tags. Part of the nonresident quota is reserved for outfitters.

For information, contact the Montana Department of Fish, Wildlife, and Parks, 1420 E. 6th, Helena, MT 59620; (406) 444-2535. For information on drawing statistics, ask for a free copy of the ANNUAL HUNTING REGULATIONS.

NATIONAL FOREST DIRECTORY FOR MONTANA
Beaverhead/Deerlodge National Forest
　420 Barrett St.
　Dillon, MT 59725-3572
　(406) 683-3900
Bitterroot National Forest
　1801 N. 1st St.
　Hamilton, MT 59840
　(406) 363-7121
Custer National Forest
　1310 Main St.
　PO Box 50760
　Billings, MT 59105
　(406) 657-6361

Flathead National Forest
1935 3rd Ave. E.
Kalispell, MT 59901
(406) 758-5200

Gallatin National Forest
Federal Building
10 E. Babcock Ave.
PO Box 130
Bozeman, MT 59771
(406) 587-6702

Helena National Forest
2880 Skyway Dr.
Helena, MT 59601
(406) 449-5201

Kootenai National Forest
506 Highway 2 W.
Libby, MT 59923
(406) 293-6211

Lewis and Clark National Forest
PO Box 869
1101 15th St. N.
Great Falls, MT 59403
(406) 791-7700

Lolo National Forest
Building 24, Ft. Missoula
Missoula, MT 59801
(406) 329-3750

Bureau of Land Management State Office
Granite Tower
222 N. 32nd St.
PO Box 36800
Billings, MT 59107-6800
(406) 255-2885

NEW MEXICO

Everything you've ever heard or read about New Mexico's elk hunting is true, if you've perceived it as a fine place to pursue big bulls. You also might have heard that the best elk hunting is on private ranches, which is only partially true. Plenty of public areas support quality elk, and all of them require a lottery draw to get a tag.

The Valle Vidal unit is the premier spot that hunters dream about. It originally was part of the famed Vermejo Ranch, but was given to the federal government as a gift. It was then incorporated into the Carson National Forest, and now offers outstanding hunting to those fortunate hunters who draw a tag. Other excellent public land hunts are on the Gila National Forest farther to the south. Plenty of roads in this region allow good access to the big bulls that roam there. As in most quality areas, a lottery draw is required.

The densest elk populations are in the north and west, with scattered herds in other areas. In the north, most elk inhabit Rio Arriba, Taos, Colfax, Mora, Los Alamos, and Sandoval counties. Catron County in the west supports the biggest herds there, and portions of Lincoln and Otero counties have good numbers of animals in the southcentral region. The Carson, Santa Fe and Gila national forests are notable public areas that have plenty of elk.

About 50,000 elk inhabit New Mexico, with an average annual harvest of about 12,000 animals. This compares to a harvest of only 2,500 animals just 15 years ago, indicating the tremendous elk explosion in the state.

Several seasons are offered each year running five days long. A hunter may apply for only one. Resident and nonresident tags are given out in a lottery draw, but landowners are given a set number of tags for their respective properties and may distribute the tags as they wish. Many ranches are managed by outfitters, and hunts are not cheap.

For information, contact the New Mexico Department of Fish and Game, PO Box 25112, Santa Fe, NM 87504; (505) 827-7911. For statistics on the lottery, request a free copy of the PUBLIC-HUNT DRAWING ODDS. New Mexico does not offer bonus or preference points.

<u>NATIONAL FOREST DIRECTORY FOR NEW MEXICO</u>
Carson National Forest
  208 Cruz Alta Rd.
  Taos, NM 87571
  (505) 758-6200
Cibola National Forest
  2113 Osuna Rd. NE, Suite A
  Albuquerque, NM 87113-1001
  (505) 761-4650
Gila National Forest
  3005 E. Camino del Bosque
  Silver City, NM 88061
  (505) 388-8201
Lincoln National Forest
  Federal Building
  1101 New York Ave.
  Alamogordo, NM 88310-6992
  (505) 434-7200
Santa Fe National Forest
  1474 Rodeo Road
  Santa Fe, NM 87505
  (505) 438-7840
Apache National Forest is in both Arizona and New Mexico. See Arizona listing.

Bureau of Land Management State Office
PO Box 27115
Santa Fe, NM 87502
(505) 438-7400

OREGON

This west coast state ranks among the top in elk numbers, with about 120,000 animals within its borders. Two major north-south mountain ranges, the Coastal Range and Cascade Range, harbor large numbers of animals, but the densest populations are in the extreme northeast.

The Roosevelt subspecies dwells in the west, while the Rocky Mountain elk lives in the central and east regions. Hunters annually take about 5,000 Roosevelt elk and 15,000 Rocky Mountain. The elk that inhabit the coastal forests are by far the toughest to hunt, not only in Oregon, but in all of the west. This exceedingly steep, densely timbered and very wet rain forest offers a tough challenge to hunters.

The heavist concentrations of elk are in three counties in the northeast: Umatilla, Union, and Wallowa. Less dense populations in that region are found in Gilliam, Morrow, Grant and Baker counties. In the central area, populations are most concentrated in Hood River County and the east portion of Lane County. All the west coast counties are equally represented with good numbers of elk. The Tioga unit in the southwest and Saddle Mountain unit in the northwest have long been popular areas. Perhaps the two most exceptional areas that hunters dream of hunting are the Starkey unit and the Strawberry region near John Day. Both these units are tough to draw, and they harbor exceptional bulls. In the northeast, the Snake River, Minam, and Imnaha units have traditionally given up plenty of good bulls.

The Umatilla and Wallowa-Whitman national forests offer plenty of public hunting in the northeast, while the Deschutes National Forest has good densities of elk near the Cascade Range. On the west coast, the Siuslaw National Forest harbors good concentrations of elk. Plenty of private paper companies own vast tracts of land, many of which are open to public hunting.

Tags are distributed according to the region and season to be hunted. Some are available in a lottery, others are offered across the counter. For information, contact the Oregon Department of Fish and Wildlife, 2501 SW 1st Ave., Portland, OR 97207; (503) 229-5410. For statistics on lottery draws, request the free report, OREGON CONTROLLED-HUNT TAG SUMMARY.

NATIONAL FOREST DIRECTORY FOR OREGON
Deschutes National Forest
  1645 Highway 20 E.
  Bend, OR 97701
  (541) 388-2715
Fremont National Forest
  524 N. G St.
  Lakeview, OR 97630
  (541) 947-2151
Malheur National Forest
  PO Box 909
  John Day, OR 97845
  (541) 575-3000
Mt. Hood National Forest
  16400 Champion Way
  Sandy, OR 97055
  (503) 668-1700
Ochoco National Forest
  3160 NE 3rd St.
  PO Box 490
  Prineville, OR 97754
  (541) 416-6500
Rogue River National Forest
  Federal Bldg., 333 W. 8th St.
  PO Box 520
  Medford, OR 97501
  (541) 858-2200

Siskiyou National Forest
 PO Box 440
 Grants Pass, OR 97526-0242
 (541) 471-6500
Siuslaw National Forest
 4077 Research Way
 Corvallis, OR 97333
 (541) 750-7000
Umatilla National Forest
 2517 SW Hailey Ave.
 Pendleton, OR 97801
 (541) 278-3716
Umpqua National Forest
 PO Box 1008
 Roseburg, OR 97470
 (541) 672-6601
Wallowa-Whitman National Forest
 PO Box 907
 Baker City, OR 97814
 (541) 523-6391
Willamette National Forest
 PO Box 10607
 Eugene, OR 97440
 (541) 465-6521
Winema National Forest
 2819 Dahlia
 Klamath Falls, OR 97601
 (541) 883-6714

Bureau of Land Management State Office
 1515 SW 5th
 PO Box 2965
 Portland, OR 97208-2965
 (503) 952-6003

UTAH

Over the last 25 years, Utah's elk population tripled in size, from less than 20,000 in 1975 to more than 60,000 today. Annual harvests run about 10,000 animals, with around 40 percent being antlerless.

Much of Utah's boom in elk herds is due to conservative hunting while herds were being allowed to expand, as well as extensive transplant programs that resulted in new herds being established in many areas.

The densest herds live in the eastern portions of Cache and Rich counties in the north, as well as in all of Morgan County, and the western portions of Rich and Summit counties, also in the north. Other highly concentrated herds are in the southern portion of Utah County, the eastern portions of Sanpete, Sevier, and Piute counties, and the western portions of Carbon, Emery, Wayne, and Garfield counties.

National forests that coincide with those herds are the Cache and Wasatch in the north, and the Dixie and Fishlake in the central areas. Plenty of BLM lands also offer excellent public hunting.

Utah has superb lottery draw units throughout the state. The Book Cliffs and Three Corners areas are my personal favorites, and other outstanding units are Monroe, Panguitch Lake, Mt. Dutton, and many others.

General season tags are unlimited for residents and nonresidents, and bonus points are awarded. For information, contact the Utah Division of Wildlife Resources, 1594 W. North Temple, Suite 2110, PO Box 146301, Salt Lake City, UT 84114-6301; (801) 538-4700. For statistics on limited entry units, request the free report, UTAH DRAWING ODDS.

NATIONAL FOREST DIRECTORY FOR UTAH

Ashley National Forest
355 N. Vernal Ave.
Vernal, UT 84078
(801) 789-1181

Dixie National Forest
82 N. 100 E.
Cedar City, UT 84720-2686
(801) 865-3700

Fishlake National Forest
115 E. 900 N.
Richfield, UT 84701
(801) 896-9233

Manti-La Sal National Forest
599 W. Price River Dr.
Price, UT 84501
(801) 636-3500

Uinta National Forest
88 W. 100 N.
Provo, UT 84601
(801) 342-5100

Wasatch-Cache National Forest
8236 Federal Bldg.
125 S. State St.
Salt Lake City, UT 84138
(801) 524-5030

Bureau of Land Management State Office
PO Box 45155
Salt Lake City, UT 84145-0155
(801) 539-4001

WASHINGTON

The smallest state in the West has the second highest human population, and continues to suffer a serious loss of habitat as civilization advances. Elk are well established, but herds are somewhat static. For almost 25 years, numbers were around 55,000. They are currently at around 60,000, suggesting that all areas are at their maximum carrying capacities.

Both Roosevelt elk and Rocky Mountain elk live in Washington, the former along the coast, and the latter in the more easterly areas. Annual harvests for each species are only about 3,000, which is half of what was taken 25 years ago.

On the Olympic Peninsula, Jefferson County has the densest numbers of elk, along with the southern portion of Clallam County and the northern portion of Grays Harbor County. In the southwest, Pacific, Cowlitz, and Wahkiakum have the greatest concentrations of animals. In the central areas, most elk live in the eastern portions of Pierce and Lewis counties, the northwest portion of Yakima County, and the northeast portion of Kittitas County. In the extreme southeast, high densities of elk can be found along the Oregon border in Walla Walla, Columbia, Garfield, and Asotin counties.

National forests that coincide with high density elk areas are the Olympic, Snowqualmie, Gifford Pinchot and the Wenatchee. Large paper company tracts are often open to public hunting as well.

Despite the rather low harvest, Washington offers some excellent lottery draw hunts. Some choice areas include Mill Creek in the Blue Mountains, the Margaret unit north of Mount St. Helens, the Toutle Unit north and west of Mount St. Helens, and Mt. Adams, West Goatrocks, and the Carlton Creek units. There are some excellent muzzleloader hunts

available. Tags are offered in a lottery.

Resident and nonresident tags are unlimited; hunters must choose only one region. Bonus points are offered for limited entry hunts. For information, contact the Washington Department of Fish and Wildlife, 600 Capitol Way N., Olympia, WA 98501; (206) 902-2200. For statistics on lottery-draw areas, send $3.00 for the HARVEST REPORT.

<u>NATIONAL FOREST DIRECTORY FOR WASHINGTON</u>
Colville National Forest
  765 S. Main
  Colville, WA 99114
  (509) 684-7000
Gifford Pinchot National Forest
  10600 NE 51st Circle
  Vancouver, WA 98682
  (360) 891-5000
Mt. Baker-Snowqualmie National Forest
  21905 64th Ave. W.
  Mountlake Terrace, WA 98043
  (425) 775-9702
Okanogan National Forest
  1240 S. 2nd Ave.
  Okanogan, WA 98840
  (509) 826-3275
Olympic National Forest
  1835 Black Lake Blvd. SW
  Olympia, WA 98512
  (360) 956-2300
Wenatchee National Forest
  215 Melody Lane
  Wenatchee, WA 98801
  (509) 662-4335

There is no BLM State Office in Washington.

WYOMING

Wyoming's elk herds have exploded over the last few decades, from around 40,000 in 1975 to more than 100,000 today. Each year, between 15,000 to 20,000 elk are taken by hunters.

The highest density areas are in Park and Teton counties which include and surround Yellowstone National Park. National forests that coincide within those areas are the Shoshone and Bridger-Teton. Other large herds live in the Bighorn Mountains, including portions of Washakie, Big Horn, Johnson, and Sheridan counties. In the Medicine Bow mountains along the Colorado border, decent herds live in the southern portions of Carbon and Albany counties.

Seasons vary widely in this state, depending on the units. Many wilderness areas open in early September to rifle hunters, while other seasons open later. Because Wyoming is sparsely populated and restricts nonresidents, hunter success is consistently among the highest in the west.

Some of the top limited entry units are south of Rock Springs, the Red Desert, Green Mountain, and the late units surrounding Yellowstone in the Cody and Sunlight Basin areas.

Resident tags are unlimited, but nonresidents must draw in a lottery with a standard application deadline of January 31. No bonus points are offered for elk. For information, contact the Wyoming Game and Fish Department, 5400 Bishop Blvd., Cheyenne, WY 82006; (307) 777-4600. For statistics on limited entry units, request the WYOMING DEMAND INDEX for $7.00.

APPENDIX

NATIONAL FOREST DIRECTORY FOR WYOMING

Bighorn National Forest
1969 S. Sheridan Ave.
Sheridan, WY 82801
(307) 672-0751

Black Hills National Forest
RR 2, Box 200
Custer, SD, 57730-9501
(605) 673-2251

Bridger-Teton National Forest
340 N. Cache
PO Box 1888
Jackson, WY 83001
(307) 739-5500

Medicine Bow-Routt National Forests
(Medicine Bow is in Wyoming and Routt is in Colorado)
2468 Jackson St.
Laramie, WY 82070-6535
(307) 745-2300

Shoshone National Forest
808 Meadow Lane
Cody, WY 82414
(307) 527-6241

Bureau of Land Management State Office
PO Box 1828
Cheyenne, WY 82003-1828
(307) 775-6256

BOOKS BY JIM ZUMBO

Books, videos and cassettes by Jim Zumbo, Hunting Editor of Outdoor Life, are available by direct mail. For current information and prices, visit Zumbo's website, http://www.jimzumbo.com.

To order or request a brochure, call 1-800-673-4868 or (307) 587-5486, or send your request and payment to Wapiti Valley Publishing Co., P.O. Box 2390, Cody, WY 82414.

AMAZING VENISON RECIPES

200 extraordinary recipes for deer, elk, moose, and other big game. Illustrated with chapters for beginning cooks, foolproof recipes for the gamiest meat, busy day recipes, information on field care, aging, marinades, and more. Comb bound. 232 pages. ISBN 0-9624025-4-0. $16.95 plus $4.00 shipping and handling.

TO HECK WITH ELK HUNTING

This book recounts 30 of Jim's favorite hunting tales. Most are humorous, but some are bizarre. You'll laugh a lot when you read Jim's confessions of the elk woods, but you'll learn plenty, too. Illustrated with Jim's photos and hilarious cartoons drawn by famed cowboy humor artist, Boots Reynolds. Hardcover. 186 pages. ISBN 0-9624025-2-4. $17.95 plus $4.00 shipping and handling.

TO HECK WITH DEER HUNTING

Packed with tales of deer hunts around the continent, from Canada to Mexico; New York to Washington. Humorous tales of several dozen hunts, of which about half are whitetails; the others about muleys and blacktails. Jim truthfully tells the stories exactly as they happened. You'll learn about deer hunting too, as he recounts his mistakes as well as his successes. Illustrated by Boots Reynolds and Jim's photos. Hardcover. 188 pages. ISBN 0-9624025-3-2. $17.95 plus $4.00 shipping and handling.

TO HECK WITH MOOSE HUNTING

America's foremost hunting author tells about his remarkable adventures from the Arctic tundra to the African veld. Besides moose, Zumbo writes about treks for caribou, antelope, sheep, goats, and other big game animals. Although written to entertain, there's plenty of instructional material as well. Illustrated with Jim's photos and outrageous cartoons drawn by cowboy humor artist, Boots Reynolds. Hardcover. 208 pages. ISBN 0-9624025-5-9. $17.95 plus $4.00 shipping and handling.

HUNTING AMERICA'S MULE DEER

Accelerated hunting pressure and increased access to hinterlands have created a new breed of mule deer—not in a biological sense, of course, but in terms of behavior. Muleys have become increasingly wary. There are still plenty of big bucks out there, but few are easily taken. This is the first book ever done on every phase of mule deer hunting, and is now a classic. Zumbo discusses the best ways to hunt them—how, when, and where to hunt all seven subspecies, from the Rocky Mountain and desert varieties to the blacktails. Plenty of photos, with valuable information on trophy hunting. Acclaimed to be the best on the subject. Hardcover. 360 pages. ISBN 0-9624025-1-6. $19.95 plus $4.00 shipping and handling.

CALLING ALL ELK

The only book on the subject of elk hunting that covers every aspect of elk vocalization. Jim calls on all his experiences to share his expertise with the reader. This book differs from others because it deals with elk hunting throughout the entire fall instead of just the bugling season. Every hunter can improve his skills, by using Zumbo's proven techniques—no matter WHEN he or she hunts. This books is jammed with tips, techniques, and photos. Softcover. 200 pages. ISBN 0-9624025-0-8. $14.95 plus $4.00 shipping and handling.

HUNT ELK

The most comprehensive book ever written on elk hunting. This 260 page hardcover describes everything you've ever wanted to know about elk - bugling, hunting in timber, late season hunting, trophy hunting, solid advice on hunting on your own or with an outfitter, and lots more. ISBN 0-83290383-3. $24.95 plus $4.00 shipping and handling.

JIM ZUMBO'S HOT OUTFITTERS LIST

The information you've always wanted! Includes names, addresses, phone numbers, description of outfitter's territory, operation, and details of Zumbo's actual hunts. 47 outfitters listed. Plus—What you absolutely must know before hiring an outfitter, examples of nightmare hunts, how to make the best of your guide, how to plan your hunt, and western big game information. Booklet, 14 pages. $9.95 plus $4.00 shipping and handling.

OTHER PRODUCTS FROM JIM ZUMBO

E-Z COW CALL

The most versatile, easy-to-use call ever invented. Attracts elk before, during, and after the bugling season. Stops spooked elk. Reassures wary elk. Also calls and stops deer, bear and coyotes. Made of soft pliable plastic and is easy to blow. Both calling edges are of different lengths to allow calls of varying pitches. $9.95 plus $4.00 shipping and handling.

E-Z COW CALL—INSTRUCTIONAL AUDIO TAPE CASSETTE

You can be a successful elk hunter. Jim Zumbo's 30-minute audio-cassette tape will reveal how and why the E-Z COW Call works on bulls and cows, reassures alarmed elk, calls elk all season long, and more. Elk are vocal year-round, and you can imitate the "chirp" made by cows, calves, and bulls. Jim Zumbo's instructional tape details when and how to use his E-Z Cow Call, a versatile tool that belongs in every elk hunter's pocket. $9.95 plus $4.00 shipping and handling.

For information on Zumbo's videos and books, and current prices, visit Zumbo's website, http://www.jimzumbo.com or call 1-800-673-4868 for a brochure.